DOUBLE PORTION

Our Inheritance

ENTERING
INTO
THE FATHER'S
PROMISE

ANDY GLOVER

©2017

Double Portion Our Inheritance - Andy Glover
Published by Andy Glover 2017

Printed in the USA

Cover design & layout by Tom Carroll

ISBN: 978-1546534105

'Double Portion Our Inheritance' is also available at www.amazon.com in Paperback and Kindle (e-book) formats.

For more details about the ministry and upcoming events, please visit the website at www.revivaltothenations.org

CONTENTS

DEDICATION

I would like to dedicate this book to those closest to me.

Gunilla, you stood by me in my darkest hour and literally lived out the promises made on our wedding day. You have always loved selflessly, always given your all, never complained and have processed every struggle in the knowledge that this too will pass. You are a warrior and have paid a high price. I love you very much and I am so thankful that you are the one walking by my side. You're the best!

Mum and Dad, as the years go by, memories become more meaningful and my love and appreciation for you grows. You gave us an inheritance that very few people have. The Gospel has been your life and now you have passed it on. Every day you have loved me and every day you have prayed for me. I thank you for everything that you have given. Being your son is a gift I will always have. You're wonderful!

Finally, I would like to dedicate this book to my dear children, **David, Josef** and **Hanna**. You are growing up into amazing people that I know will one day impact your generation. Each one of you is a gift to us and to the world. You each carry an inheritance on your lives and my prayer for you is that every part of God's destiny will be fulfilled in your lives. You are treasures in the Kingdom.

ACKNOWLEDGEMENTS

A number of ministries, ministers and individuals acted as guides when we faced our greatest challenge. Our appreciation goes out to our board of directors, both in America and the UK, who encouraged us to rest when we needed it the most.

I am deeply indebted to the late Jack Frost of Shiloh Place Ministries, who totally undid us with the message of "Spiritual Slavery to Spiritual Sonship," and I owe so much to Catch The Fire, (formerly known as Toronto Airport Christian Fellowship) for consistency in the message of the Father's love; the love and the presence of God has met us many times when we have visited.

Thanks to Wayne and Irene Negrini for their consistent encouragement and wisdom, and to Ed Piorek for imparting the Father's Love into our hearts that it may be "the Love that sends us."

I would also like to acknowledge the writings of authors Brennan Manning and Henri Nouwen. They have brought to us amazing inspiration and helped us discover that intimacy with God is rightfully ours to have. These teachings provided a time of self-discovery, impartation and healing as wave after wave of His Love broke into our hearts.

I would also like to acknowledge my dear friend Melissa Rogers, of Tuscaloosa, Alabama, who along with her husband, Jonathan, traveled with me throughout Liberia and Ghana gathering much of the content for this book. Melissa graciously offered the gifts God has given her to compile notes from our travels, sermons, and our own conversations to place the message that was on my heart into its first written format. For her assistance I am so grateful!

We are very thankful for our connection with Fatherheart Ministries. The anointing that is on Fatherheart Ministries has had a deep and profound impact on our lives in recent years. Thank you, James and Denise Jordan, for being willing to walk out the revelation of the Father's love and share it in such a meaningful way.

Many thanks and deep appreciation to Stephen Hill who has helped make this book a reality. You understood my heart and were able to bring that to life in this book. I so value who God has made you to be and all that you carry. Our growing friendship was a key and I'm thankful for the time we got to spend together in New Zealand. Thanks for your time.

FOREWORD BY STEPHEN HILL

Whether we realise it or not, the Body of Christ worldwide is in the process of the greatest transition in its entire history. There is a massive sea-change going on, prophetically, in our understanding of the nature and character of God. This new day that is being heralded by prophetic ministries is a dawning of the revelation that God is love (that is His DNA) and that God is our Father. The purpose of Jesus' life, death, resurrection and His life now is to lead us back to His Father as sons and daughters. The purpose of the Holy Spirit's ministry is, more than anything else, to pour out the love of God within our hearts, crying "Abba, Father!" (Romans 5:5; Galatians 4:6)

God has been restoring us back to the true Gospel and the life experienced by Jesus, the apostles and the early Church. This true Gospel became obscured by false understandings of God and by legalism. Throughout history, the Holy Spirit has been uncovering what the authentic Gospel is. The Reformation uncovered the fact that we are justified, not by works, but by faith. A few centuries later, the Pentecostal and Charismatic movements highlighted again the reality of the experience of the baptism of the Holy Spirit.

All this has been wonderful, but it still wasn't the complete picture.

In our day, the Holy Spirit is revealing the missing factor. This missing factor is foundational to everything that Christianity is intended to be. The source of *everything* is the love of the Father. When we encounter the Father's love and begin to live in it, our spiritual eyes are opened to see differently.

Until I experienced it, I had no idea how the love of God would change my way of seeing everything. Now I see God in a different light, I see myself and others in a different light, and I see creation in a different light. But, probably the biggest change of all is how I read the Bible. When you get to know the personality of the Author and have the substance of His love within you, the Scriptures will make sense to you in ways that they could never do when you were just trying your best to please and serve God.

When the two disciples walked with Jesus on the road to Emmaus (Luke 24: 27), at first they did not realise who He was. Luke then writes that, during their conversation, "… And beginning with Moses and all the Prophets, he interpreted to them in all the Scripture the things concerning himself." Yes! The resurrected Jesus opens up *all* the Scriptures to reveal New Covenant realities.

Andy Glover's book brings us new perspectives on sonship in the Scriptures. Andy and Gunilla have walked a real journey in the past few years, a journey of opening their hearts to the love of the Father, seeing it transform their hearts, their marriage, and their ministry. They are heralds and evangelists of the Father's love. Operating out of the love of God, they incarnate fatherhood and motherhood, which the world desperately needs. This book will open your eyes to grasp the wonderful inheritance that God has in store for His beloved sons and daughters.

— STEPHEN HILL, TAUPO, NEW ZEALAND, 2017

Stephen Hill is part of Fatherheart Ministries and is the author of *Primal Hope: Finding Confidence Beyond Religion, Creating a Shape for Life to Flow*, and *John: A Prophetic Revelation*.

INTRODUCTION

A group of businessmen in Redding, California, were once asked a simple question: "What is the biggest problem in the world today?"[1] After some thought and deliberation they came back with a consensus. The most menacing problem facing the world today is the problem of *fatherlessness*.

Some would assert that *almost every* social ill faced by America's children is related to fatherlessness. The statistics confirm this. From drug abuse to teenage pregnancy, and from poverty to crime, the story is profoundly clear. Within our cultures, not only in America but also around the world, the issue of *fatherlessness* lies at the heart of much that worries us about contemporary society.

What is especially troubling about this is that, even within so-called 'Christian' nations, such as America, which have a high percentage of church-goers, the problem *still* exists. Recent studies reveal that the divorce rates among

---

1. *"The Consequences of Fatherlessness"* on www.fathers.com, National Centre for Fathering, 02 June 2013.

believers are the *same* as those of unbelievers.[2] This shows that there is a huge disconnection between what we *say* we believe and what we are able to *live out* in our daily lives. We have become experts in judging the problems of others but cannot receive healing and change in our own hearts.

The last few years of my life have been a major season of enlightenment. The Father's love has ravished my heart, turned me inside out, and changed what I was powerless in my own strength to alter. My life, marriage, family and ministry have gone through a seismic renaissance. Before this new enlightenment I was fatherless in my heart. I lived like an orphan, not knowing or understanding who Abba really was.

In John 14:6, Jesus declares, "I am the way the truth and the life, no one comes to the Father except through me." I had read this verse many times but never realized what it really meant. I was saved, I knew that my sins were forgiven and that I was going to heaven. I knew how to preach, heal the sick and cast out demons. I thought I had it all. But I was so enamored with my own success that I was blind to what I lacked. I knew Jesus and the Holy Spirit, but something was still missing.

My growing awareness that something was profoundly

---

2. *"New Marriage and Divorce Statistics"* on www.barna.com, The Barna Group Ltd., 2009.

missing started me on a spiritual journey. I began to look afresh at Jesus and at His relationship with His Father, whom He called "Abba." I knew from reading the Bible that God loved me but the problem was that I had very little *experience* of that love. My marriage and family life were proof enough of that. Without this full revelation of the Father's love in my heart I related to others in ways that were controlling and filled with anger. More than anything, I was constantly striving to live in such a way as to never be vulnerable before God or man.

If our theology is not teaching us about the love of the Father and His desire to live in us, then there is a problem with our theology. Jesus came with a very clear mandate and that was to be *the Way to the Father.* He called Himself 'the Door' (John 10:9), giving us a simple clue to what He intended for us all—a wonderful invitation into the Father's heart.

In 2005, I was given some CDs by the late Jack Frost on spiritual slavery and spiritual sonship. Jesus used these teachings to finally break open my heart of pain. After listening to them, I took the bull by the horns in order to pursue what was missing in my heart. I knew that I had received a small taste of the love of God. In the ensuing few years, I learned to open my heart and allowed the Father to find me.

My prayer for you, as you read through this book, is that you will receive grace to *let go*. Letting go is easier said than done, however it is the Father who draws us. It is *His* work and we get the opportunity to participate in what He does. As you read, may your heart be captivated and caught by His furious love.

— ANDY GLOVER, MALMO, 2017

PART ONE

THE PROPHETIC
MANDATE

CHAPTER ONE

THE AGAPE REFORMATION

~

The love of the law will only lead to deeper bondage; only love will change our hearts.

Looking back on it now, 2005 was undoubtedly one of our toughest years. Gunilla and I were living in Ghana, West Africa, where we had been for the previous three years. The reality of life in this challenging environment was getting to us and we were struggling with the pressure of our personal circumstances. Our marriage was under strain from living and ministering in a third world environment. Issues that we had managed to keep hidden for many years began to surface.

One day during this time, Gunilla shocked me by

telling me that she wasn't sure that she loved me anymore. This admission really rocked my world and raised more questions than answers. The truth is, I was a very driven and controlling individual. I had to be obeyed and knew how to exert the right amount of pressure on Gunilla so that I always got what I wanted. Our relationship had become very co-dependent, with Gunilla being afraid to upset me. In addition to this, and because I found it very heard to express heart-intimacy, I had begun to be drawn to pornographic websites, especially when I felt any sort of rejection or abandonment. Unknown to me, I was in a desperate search for real intimacy. Our children had a father who was only partially present, my relationship with them being shallow. I lacked the ability to give them what they really needed. I loved them and wanted them to be safe but I found it very difficult to express love. I was dysfunctional and I had no idea how I got there or how to get free.

The reality of our lives is revealed through the fruit that we produce. My relationships showed me very clearly that something was broken in my heart and I had no power to fix it. Bad fruit meant the root was not good. Jesus says it this way:

> *"Either make the tree good and its fruit good,*
> *or else make the tree bad and its fruit bad; for*
> *a tree is known by its fruit."*
>
> — MATTHEW 12:33

I knew that I loved Gunilla, deep down in my heart. We had seen God's hand in our relationship and His calling upon us as a couple was evident. But I also knew it was time for me to resolve some deeper issues in my heart. Then a good friend gave me a series of teaching by the late Jack Frost on "Spiritual Sonship." This was the catalyst for a profound shift in my life.

As I listened to the messages, my curiosity was roused. My heart began to open and little drops of the Father's love began to gently pour over me. As I listened to Jack's testimony I began to weep. It was as though he was speaking directly to my heart. I kept returning back to those stories because I so enjoyed the inner relief and hope they implanted in my heart. Up to that point in my life, I had blamed the devil for my problems. It is easy to blame someone else and avoid personal responsibility for our own stuff. Deliverance ministry is undoubtedly important, however, if we don't have a personal revelation of the Father's love, our core belief system remains unchanged.

After going through Jack Frost's series a few times, I came to the shocking realization that I had an orphan heart. I was living and thinking like an orphan. Simply put, an orphan is a child whose parents are dead or whose parents have permanently abandoned them. I was living as believer, yet I did not know God as my *Father*. I started to acquaint myself with books and CDs, and attended conferences relating to the Father's love. By the end of 2005, I had embarked on my journey into the heart of the Father.

By the time February 2006 came around, things had slowly started to change as I began to discover that God was actually my Father. Our ministry board suggested that we take a six-month sabbatical at our home in California. It was a relatively easy decision to take a period of leave; we desperately needed a rest. From June through December 2006, we took a sabbatical. Sabbaticals are not easy for Type A personalities like me. When you are accustomed to being proactive and fully engaged in life, being still and waiting on the Lord can be difficult, to say the least.

Throughout this period of time I began to discover what it meant to receive the Father's love. For many hours, I would sit with instrumental worship music playing in the background and simply ask the Father to love me. At first, it was an intense struggle to disengage myself from the world and listen to the Father, but over time He softened my heart. For weeks and weeks I would sit and receive what felt like liquid love pouring through a funnel into my heart. My heart was being restored, past hurts were being healed; I was beginning to come to grips with the simple fact that the Father loves me just for who I am, not what I can do for him. The feeling inside me, that told me I could never do enough, was beginning to disappear. This encounter with the Father's love was turning my heart inside out.

For me, this was the beginning of what I call my "Agape Reformation." I heard Jack Frost preach a message on "The Agape Reformation" in 2006 in Toronto. This reformation of my heart was transforming my relationships and my marriage, as well as my approach to the ministry I was called to. My entire life, past, present and future, was engulfed in the love of the Father. My prophetic destiny was sealed by this love. This all happened for the simple reason that my heart was being reformed by love. This was a love that I had only heard about but had never actually experienced for myself. Now I was beginning to experience it and I have not looked back since.

Before going any further, I need to lay the foundation for why I believe the love of the Father is so profoundly important for today. I am convinced that we are in a paramount moment in the history of the nations. This current season is not just the product of natural progression but one destined before the beginning of time. God appointed you and me to walk the earth at this point in history for a specific reason. What is more, God has a distinct message for this season. Just as the time was appointed for Jesus to come, for the Holy Spirit to descend at Pentecost, for the apostles to carry the message throughout the earth, for Martin Luther to bring revelation of God's gift of grace, and for a revival to break loose on Azusa Street, so there is a revelation that God is releasing from the throne of heaven to His church in this present age.

I am not one of those doomsday prophets waiting for the earthquake or the tsunami to hit the coast of California and begin some sort of cataclysmic apocalypse. That's not what I'm looking for! I have read enough of Scripture to know that God is not through with Planet Earth. So, you can remove your life jackets because God is not finished with this place yet! God is wanting to raise up a generation of sons and daughters on the earth today; sons and daughters that carry the heart of their Father to bring a heavenly mandate to earth. Sons who know their Father and whose ultimate purpose is to bring restoration and hope back to the broken.

As sons come forth, they will come forth with the heart and passion of the Father to see His kingdom manifest on earth. Sons of God, who understand the identity and inheritance bestowed on them, also understand their authority in the Kingdom. That authority, however, is made manifest in a desire to bring the surrounding brokenness back into God's order. Only sons have that authority because of the relationship they have with the Father, just as Jesus' authority derived from His relationship with the Father (John 5:19). This redemptive mandate is part of the message that God desires to be proclaimed for this generation.

For many years I believed that my sonship was connected with my performance or my ability to behave in a certain way. My view was similar to that of the lost son who on his way home rehearses what he will say when he meets his father: "Make me like one of your hired servants." (Luke 15:19) In my heart I had not caught the real meaning of redemption, for the very simple reason that I had not encountered the Father. It was for this purpose that I was saved; that I may be redeemed back to the Father, not as an adopted child or a servant but *as a son*. We were created as His, conceived in His heart before the foundation of the world. Our redemption is simply our journey back to our source, the Father. (Ephesians 1:4)

I am so thankful for Trevor Galpin of Fatherheart Ministries, and others, who have helped me understand the historical background to Galatians 4:4-6. "Setting a son in place" is the correct concept as opposed to the contemporary concept of "adoption" as we understand it in the Western world.[3] That wrong understanding of the meaning of "adoption" has led many of us to believe that we were not His from the beginning. In a personal way the story of the "lost son," in Luke 15:11-22, highlights a father who lost a son and was able to redeem that same son back. The father in the parable never stopped loving despite the orphaned hearts of both his sons. The parable clearly reveals the heart of the Father to redeem and "set in place" his sons whom

---

3. Many English translations of the Bible have rendered the Greek word '*huiothesia*' (meaning 'to place as a son') as 'adoption.' This has led to widespread confusion as to the real meaning of the Scripture. Bible translations in other languages generally do not use the word 'adoption' to describe '*huiothesia*.'

He has always loved.

In this book, we are going to look at the incredible relationship that existed between Elijah and Elisha. We will see how the relationship between these two prophets is very relevant to the revelation of sonship and the Father's heart. Elisha not only acquired the prophetic anointing of Elijah but he stepped right into his prophetic destiny as a *son* of Elijah. God was after Elisha's heart, and God is after your heart too!

Let us begin in the book of Malachi:

> *"Behold, I will send Elijah the prophet before the coming of the great and dreadful day of the Lord."*
>
> — MALACHI 4:5

This statement *"the great and dreadful day of the Lord"* is another way of saying that *"...the Kingdom of God is at hand."* (Mark 1:15). It is not a proclamation of coming calamity; it is saying the Kingdom of God is *here*. The Greek word for 'kingdom' is *'basileia'* which simply means God's right to rule and reign. This, then, is a declaration that God's kingdom is breaking in. Malachi is using Old Testament language to describe the coming of the Kingdom. The coming of the Holy Spirit into and upon our lives is an expression of the Kingdom.

Malachi says:

> *"Behold, I will send Elijah the prophet before*
> *the coming of the great and dreadful day of*
> *the Lord and He will turn the hearts of the*
> *Fathers to the children and the hearts of the*
> *children unto the fathers, lest I come and*
> *strike the earth with a curse."*

— MALACHI 4:5,6

Malachi foretells that a great prophet will arrive on earth before the coming of the Messiah, before the coming of the Kingdom of God; a great prophet who will walk in the power and spirit of Elijah. This prophet will come like Elijah with a *fathering spirit*. The fathering spirit will restore and reconcile the hearts of fathers to their children, and children to their fathers. Malachi is not saying that Elijah himself will come; Elijah had already been taken up in a chariot of fire by a whirlwind sent from heaven. (2 Kings 2:11). We now know that this prophecy was partially fulfilled through the ministry of John the Baptist, who came preaching in the wilderness of Judea, "Repent, for the Kingdom of heaven is at hand!" (Matthew 11:13-15)

Both Elijah and John the Baptist prophetically announced the coming of the King. Both these men had ministries that were marked by a restoration that was taking place through their lives. This uniting of the heart between father and son is exemplified in the relationship between Elijah and Elisha. It is also reflected in the words the Father spoke to Jesus when John was baptizing Him in the Jordan River. At that point, Jesus knew that He was favored by the Father. He knew why He was sent to this earth—to carry out the Father's will and bring revelation of the Father and His love.

Now think about this for a moment; God spoke through Malachi that the Elijah Spirit was to come prior to the Messiah's first coming. John the Baptist was an Elijah-type forerunner heralding the coming of Jesus. This Elijah Spirit and the restoration of the Father's heart preceded the first coming of Christ. Similarly, God desires that this same Elijah Spirit will precede the second coming of Christ. When the Father spoke forth from the clouds from heaven, "This is my beloved Son, in whom I am well pleased," He affirmed His love and acceptance into the heart of Jesus. The Father wants to bestow the same revelation and identity upon the Church today; a revelation of who the Father really is so that we would know and understand His presence and His love.

Throughout the history of the Church, God has been revealing Himself progressively. Five hundred years ago, the Reformation revealed that the just shall live by faith. Martin Luther's revelation of justification by faith inspired a whole generation and ushered in a new season for the Church. Then, at the start of the 20th Century, the Azusa

Street outpouring in Los Angeles again moved the Church into a new season. The Baptism of the Holy Spirit was rediscovered, the gifts of the Spirit were reignited, and a fresh enlightenment of the power of the Holy Spirit was revealed. Like the Great Reformation, this movement has affected the entire earth. Salvation by grace is being preached and the power of the Spirit is being felt in every nation.

I would like to suggest that we are in the midst of another reformation; an *Agape Reformation*. During this season, the Church will, once again, discover who the Father really is and experience His tenderness and love. Consequently, the Body of Christ will live as sons and daughters who are basking in the love of the Father. The Church will have a full knowledge of the triune God—Father, Son and Holy Spirit. God wants to reveal Himself totally throughout the earth, preparing the way for the second coming of Christ and the ushering in of His Kingdom on earth as it is in heaven.

During this Agape Reformation we are going to see God's loving presence released upon the Church in new ways, with fresh manifestations of the miraculous that reveal the Father. The fullness of the Spirit of Elijah, as prophesied in Malachi 4:4-5, will infiltrate the hearts of God's people who will, like Elijah, operate as true prophets. The sons of God will see, bless, enhance, and restore God's redemptive purposes on the earth. There will be a renewed revelation of God the Father's love for the Church. Spiritual orphans will be awakened to their identity as sons and daughters of the King.

When the Church fully grasps this inheritance, freely given to us as God's children, then the world will see who God is and what His plan is for this earth. Only then can we truly reflect the reality of who God the Father is, bringing a deeper revelation of salvation to the nations. Then our hearts will be made one with the Father in such a way that we will only say and do what *the Father* is saying and doing. During the Agape Reformation, God the Father will totally consume our hearts with His fiery love!

This Agape Reformation is already sweeping across the nations. In Toronto, Canada, there has been an outpouring of the Father's love since 1994. I visited Toronto for the first time that same year. In the early days of the Toronto outpouring many were critical, saying that the manifestations were either of the devil or the flesh. However, those with courage to really seek after God soon discovered that many who were being outwardly touched were also having profound inner encounters with the Father. The evidence that God was moving was confirmed by testimonies that spoke of deep and impacting encounters in which men and women experienced the love of the Father.

Until we have experienced God's love it is impossible to know what it really is. Our concept of love is filtered through our own experiences as though we are wearing sunglasses that shield the full radiance of His light. Often we paint a picture of our own father or mother over the face of God. The level of trust and intimacy we have experienced with our parents is the level of trust and intimacy with which we engage our heavenly Father. Unfortunately, aspects of our relationships with our parents, such as fear or shame, can also prove to be destructive in our ability to receive God's agape love.

God, however, is after our hearts. The Agape Reformation is happening *now*. God's redemptive purposes for this earth have not changed. The time has come to reveal the fullness of who He is so that we can reflect that to the world. God desires to come in a deeply personal way to His Church so that we will cry out, "Abba, Daddy!" (Romans 8:15) God wants to consume our hearts, to have us as His own, and to establish His Kingdom on earth as it is in heaven. This generation must ready itself to encounter the Father like never before.

As you read this book, I encourage you to begin your journey towards discovering the Father's love with this prayer:

> *Father, in Jesus' name, I ask that You would reveal Yourself to me and that You would begin to overwhelm my heart with Your love. Amen.*

CHAPTER TWO

THE SPIRIT
OF ELIJAH

~

*Our greatest need is not more power,
anointing or even gifting...It is simply that
we would know God as our father.*

Elijah the prophet is one of the most significant men in
the Bible. He was one of only two men who escaped
death (the other being Enoch) so it stands to reason that
there is something we should learn from Elijah's relationship
with the Father. The power of God manifested through
Elijah, in both the miraculous and the spoken prophetic
word, was so deeply rooted within the heart of Israel that
even Jesus Himself, the Messiah, was mistaken for the
prophet Elijah (Matthew 16:14). Elijah appeared alongside
Moses with Christ on the Mount of Transfiguration (Luke

9:28-36). Some even speculate that he is one of the two witnesses described in Revelation 11:1-14.

As I meditate upon the biblical story of Elijah and what Scripture says about him, there is no doubt that his gifting reflected a more profound reason for his calling and ministry. His life impacted a generation and those who walked alongside him desired a father-son-relationship with him. But we can be so taken in by signs that we can often miss the purpose for them.

What is the Spirit of Elijah? What does the authoritative anointing that enveloped Elijah's life have to do with our connection to the Father's heart?

Let me suggest that we, the Body of Christ, are *now* carrying the Spirit of Elijah! Let's take a look again at Malachi 4:5-6:

> *"Behold, I will send you Elijah the prophet*
> *before the coming of the great and dreadful*
> *day of the Lord. And he will turn the hearts*
> *of the fathers to the children and the hearts of*
> *the children to their fathers, lest I come and*
> *strike the earth with a curse."*

This scripture has proven to be true for me in a very personal way. When the Father started to break into my heart with His love, one of my cries was to find a father figure. I desired someone that I could relate to, someone who was further along the road than myself and who understood what a father was really meant to be. I had been around a lot of anointed and gifted leaders, but I had found very few people in ministry with a genuine heart to father others. I just wanted to be loved for who I was and not for what I could do in ministry. I truly wanted someone in my life that could speak straight to the core of my heart.

Then, in 2000, Gunilla and I met Wayne and Irene Negrini. I was blown away when I first met them. They were different and somewhat odd but they were open and real. What is more, they had a genuine heart to love those who the Lord brought their way. It took a while, however, to really connect with them. Because of the struggles of my heart throughout 2004 and 2005, I avoided them; they could see right through me and that was too much for me. Then, in 2006, the Holy Spirit reconnected us and it was the best thing that happened to me. Today, Gunilla and I look up to them as they love, affirm, encourage, and bless us. They are truly amazing people. They truly are an expression of my heavenly Father to me and they carry the Elijah Spirit.

I want to highlight three specific aspects of the Elijah anointing:

Firstly, Elijah's identity as a prophet;

Secondly, Elijah's fathering spirit;

Thirdly, Elijah's mandate to bring restoration.

These three attributes of the Elijah Spirit are profoundly important in understanding God's destiny for our individual lives. More than that, they are vital in order to recognize God's prophetic destiny for the entire universe. The Elijah anointing is destined for your heart and life, and it is immersing itself within God's people across the nations, beckoning hearts to turn towards the Father.

1. The first thing about Elijah is that he was **a prophet**. That is a well known fact. However, we need to understand the nature of Elijah's prophetic ministry. As I mentioned in the previous chapter, there is a distorted interpretation in the Church today about what prophetic gifting really is. Elijah wasn't remotely interested in having a title or gaining popularity. He was out to call God's people into alignment with God's heart. This is the nature of a true prophet. Authentic prophets see into the spiritual realm and recognize God's desire and solution for the surrounding circumstances. In other words, they see what is happening and provide God's answer.

Seeing into the spiritual realm must come from a deep,

intimate, relationship with the Father in which the prophet's heart meshes together with the heart of God. As we journey deeper into the heart of the Father, and this prophetic gifting becomes manifest, we will be able to see what is happening in our own lives and can then speak out God's solution to that situation. That is *true* prophetic gifting and prophetic anointing. That was the prophetic anointing on Elijah's life.

Daddy's love softens our hearts to hear correctly so that we can operate in the prophetic. Our ears and eyes are opened to hear and see the Father, and in turn we operate as the Father does here on earth. The prophetic gifting and anointing flows from a heart tenderized by the Father's love.

2. Secondly, Elijah had a **fathering spirit.** Malachi prophesied that the one who would come in the spirit of Elijah would "...*turn the hearts of the fathers to the children and the hearts of the children to their fathers.*" Elijah was a *father.* Scripture doesn't record that he was a natural, biological father, however, he was a *spiritual* father. He operated in alignment with the Father heart of God, *especially* in his relationship with Elisha. Fathers reproduce who they are in the lives of their children. Elijah reproduced what he received from His own Father, God.

The world today is desperate for fathering. Almost every problem that humanity faces is traceable to a lack of parenting. In the New Testament, there are two things that God asks for us to pray for more of; firstly, we should pray for more workers into the harvest field (Matthew 9:38), *and* we should pray for more *fathers*, because there is a deficit of fathers (1 Corinthians 4:15). I believe these two prayers are connected. The workers in the harvest field need to be *fathers*, for that is what the world so badly needs.

A study by the United Kingdom Ministry of Justice found that approximately 53% of all prison inmates have grown up without their biological fathers.[4] That statistic only accounts for those who actually got involved in crime. The study didn't even look at depression, educational failure, child abuse, and the other social tragedies that are connected to an orphan heart.

These are serious problems in society but the problem of an orphan heart runs much deeper than this. Spiritual orphans cannot become spiritual fathers; it is only sons who can become spiritual fathers. I am not referring to a person who has no earthly parents; I'm talking about someone who feels and acts as if they don't belong, who lives independently without a revelation of God as their real father. A person who has no sense of identity or purpose will produce entire generations of orphans like themselves.

---

4.   Kim Williams, Vea Papadopoulou, Natalie Booth, *"Prisoners' Childhood and Family Backgrounds."* on www.gov.uk, United Kingdom Ministry of Justice, March 2012.

This is what has happened historically, and now we have an entire generation of orphans running our planet. This is why it is so important to allow the Father to deal with our hearts and set them free, so that we will be restored as His sons and daughters.

One evening in Toronto, I heard a man by the name of Ken Gott speak. He gave a call for ministry for those whose children were not following the Lord and I responded. As I walked to the front of the auditorium I saw a picture of my son Josef, standing alone on a football field. I could feel the pain of his loneliness as if it was inside my own heart. As I was seeing this vision, Fred and Sharon Wright, the former leaders of Partners in Harvest, began praying over me. The ministry of their prayers flowed through my soul and I began to weep. The pain of knowing that my son was suffering so deeply became very real. All of a sudden, I realized that the person in the vision was not Josef at all, but *me. I* was the lonely soul searching for a father.

Something incredibly deep occurred in my life that night. I fell to the ground and lay there for an extended time. When I finally stood up I realized that I was still in the vision but there was no pain attached to it. My heart had been healed and restored back to the Father. However, the truth did not escape me, that if I was struggling so intensely in my relationship to the Father, my son Josef must be struggling as well.

As we look intently at the relationship between Elijah and Elisha, we see that walking as a son is vital to becoming a father. I had to learn this truth myself as I was receiving revelation of the Father's love. It was clear to me that during the early years of our children's lives I really struggled with being a father, and it was because I did not know what it was to be a son. I was living like an orphan, filled with shame, fear and a deep insecurity that made me addicted to control. I had no understanding of the identity and inheritance bestowed upon me as a child of God. Orphans produce orphans, and I was reproducing who I was. As a result, my entire generational line was at risk.

We reproduce who we are, not only in our own children, but in the people we minister to or are connected with. We cannot help it because it is the natural consequence of life. I was living like an orphan and I automatically reproduced who I was. Only when the deepest places of my heart began to be healed did I start to see healing and restoration in my family.

Elijah knew that he was a son of God and he was able to reproduce that identity in his spiritual son, Elisha. As a result, Elisha walked with greater power, authority and influence than Elijah before him. The Elijah spirit is a fathering spirit bestowed upon sons.

3. The third thing about the Elijah anointing is the call **to restore**. Elijah was a **restorer.** He wanted to restore things back to the way God had designed and destined for them to be. Because the true prophet sees with God's eyes, he doesn't see the calamity. The true prophet sees the broken pieces formed together again and transformed into a whole new creation. In the DNA of every prophet is this desire to see things restored to the way that God originally designed them to be (Jeremiah 1:10). From that perspective, the prophet is able to speak out God's heart and see miraculous change occurring to bring the earth into alignment with the Kingdom of God.

This anointing of restoration is demonstrated again and again in Elijah's life. It compelled him to pray for rain to fall upon the parched land. As he prayed, the sky was filled with black clouds and heavy winds brought a terrific rainstorm (2 Kings 18-41-46). It is also why the word of Elijah provided more than enough oil and flour to take care of the needs of the widow (2 Kings 17:8-16). It is why he was used to bring the woman's son back to life (2 Kings 17:17-24). Even Elijah's mighty deed on Mount Carmel was a demonstration of his anointing to bring restoration. Through the spoken word given to him by God, he called down fire from heaven and initiated God's justice throughout the land (2 Kings 18).

All this was only possible because of Elijah's deep relationship with the Father. Elijah heard and saw what his Father was doing, and he responded in complete obedience.

Elijah walked as a son, and as result received an inheritance of power and anointing from God, his Father.

The three dimensions of the Spirit that were manifested through Elijah's life are that he was a true prophet, that he was a spiritual father, and that he was a restorer. I believe that the spirit and power of Elijah will be released on the Church in these last days with a force the like of which has never been seen or heard before. The Body of Christ will, once again, be a true prophetic voice, both individually and corporately. We will see what the Father is doing and, like Jesus, follow Him as our Father. In the same way that Elijah was a father, we too will live as fathers throughout this earth and we will see lives restored.

God's heart is consistently towards restoration, therefore the five-fold ministries should move the Body of Christ toward restoration:

> And He Himself gave some to be apostles, some
> prophets, some evangelists, and some pastors
> and teachers, for the equipping of the saints
> for the work of ministry, for the edifying of the
> body of Christ, till we all come to the unity of
> the faith and of the knowledge of the Son of
> God, to a perfect man, to the measure of the
> stature of the fullness of Christ; that we should
> no longer be children, tossed to and fro and

*carried about with every wind of doctrine, by
the trickery of men, in the cunning craftiness
of deceitful plotting, but, speaking the truth
in love, may grow up in all things into Him
who is the head—Christ— from whom the
whole body, joined and knit together by what
every joint supplies, according to the effective
working by which every part does its share,
causes growth of the body for the edifying of
itself in love.*

— EPHESIANS 4:11-16

It is profoundly important that we, as the Church, understand our part in God's great redemptive purpose. God has
called His Church (Ephesians 3:10) to co-participate with
Him in displaying who He is. This includes the coming
of the power and anointing of the Elijah Spirit into the
Church to be a prophetic voice; to walk as sons and mature
into fathers who can reveal the heart of Father God to the
nations, speaking forth restoration to this broken planet.
This will make more sense as we look more closely at the
relationship that existed between Elijah and Elisha because
it mirrors the relationship between God and the Church.

A profound encounter occurred between Elijah and
Elisha when Elijah was taken to heaven. (2 Kings 2). As
Elijah was taken up in the whirlwind, his mantle fell to
the ground and Elisha took it up. Something deeply

significant occurred in Elisha's life at that point, something which is a vivid prophetic picture of what happened to Jesus in Luke 3:21-22. The Spirit of God came upon Jesus and the heavenly voice said: "You are my beloved Son in whom I am well pleased." The parallels between the two events are incredible for those who have eyes to see. The encounter between Elijah and Elisha happened right at the Jordan River, the *same place* where Jesus had an encounter with *His* Father. Jesus was baptized, received confirmation and identity through the spoken word of God, and was propelled into His earthly ministry.

This coming of the anointing of God the Father is destined for your heart. It is destined for God's Church today. The Elijah Spirit is coming to sweep across the earth and bring fresh revelation of who God is and what His prophetic destiny is for this earth. The spirit of Elijah is coming. In fact, it is *already* here, paving the way for the Kingdom of God to come in its full glory!

CHAPTER THREE

THE DOUBLE PORTION

～

Our sonship is never dependent on our performance, rather it is to do with our ability to receive, accept and believe the intimate words of our Father saying to us, "I love you, my son."

When we look at the relationship between Elijah and Elisha there is a remarkable parallel with the New Covenant relationship between Jesus Christ and His Church. As I shared previously, when Jesus was being baptized in the Jordan River and Father God spoke from heaven, "This is my beloved son in whom I am well pleased," there was an affirming of identity that formed the launchpad for Jesus' earthly ministry. It was a similar affirmation of identity that occurred in Elisha's life, propelling him into his purpose and destiny. The Father desires to bestow this same identity and destiny into *our* hearts.

Everyone has their own definition of what identity actually is. In reality, identity speaks to the very core of our being when all the peripheral influences of the world are stripped away. It can be difficult to discover our true identity but God desires to make this very simple for us if we will just open up our hearts to Him.

When it comes to our spiritual identity, we can easily develop the mindset of a servant. We don't understand our identity as a son or daughter of God the Father and, as a result, we function as if we are orphans, or servants. In the depths of our hearts we believe that we do not deserve anything so we strive to try and *achieve* our inheritance. Orphans cannot receive any inheritance. *Inheritance only comes to sons.* To put it another way, prophetic destiny only comes to sons. When I lived in Africa I witnessed this firsthand. Throughout West Africa, wealthy families have big properties situated inside large compounds. In addition, there are small buildings inside the compound that are referred to as "boys' quarters." Be sure of this, however, the inheritance of the family *only* passes to the children. Everything goes to the children and nothing goes to the servants. No matter how hard the servants work to prove their loyalty they receive nothing of the inheritance. They are only looked after during their time of service.

Before I experienced the Father's love, I kept trying to force things to happen in my life, my family, and ministry. I felt that I needed to prove my loyalty, demonstrate my sacrifice, and earn a pat on the back from God. I was striving very hard to reach my inheritance and to attain my prophetic destiny. This struggle required such incredible amounts of energy that it nearly broke my relationship with my family and with God. I was always wondering why I could never have my inheritance. On the one hand, I was receiving vision and prophetic insight about my destiny but I knew that I wasn't in it! I perceived my destiny, I knew where I was *meant* to be, but it just wasn't happening.

Finally, it dawned on me. I was focused on trying to formulate my identity through what I *did* instead of receiving my identity through an encounter with the Father. Instead of letting the Father show me how much He loved me, I was assessing how hard I was working and monitoring my level of sacrifice. The harder I worked for God the better I felt about myself. As soon as I relaxed, I stopped feeling good about myself. Then God revealed to me why this happened. As soon as I would take a rest from the never-ending pressures of ministry my identity would be challenged. Suddenly I would feel lost, unworthy and unapproved. Then I would start frantically working again, not from a heart rooted in joy and peace, but out of obligation and guilt. Something had to change.

It took God's mighty hand to bring the change that I so desperately needed. He needed to grab hold of me and break into my heart in order to open my eyes to see the orphan spirit operating within me. I was living like a mere servant and it was shielding me from the very inheritance that God had already revealed to me. God said to me, "Andy, you will never formulate your identity by what you do. Your identity comes from an encounter with Me." That revelation brought a freedom unlike anything I had ever experienced.

Our identity is never found in what we do. Sonship is never derived from what we do. The words of the Father to Jesus, "You are my beloved Son in whom I am well pleased." gave Him everything He needed for ministry. Up to that pivotal point in Jesus' life, He had done *nothing*. When the Father declared His favor over Jesus, He had not even begun His earthly ministry. He had lived for years as a son to His earthly father and mother, Joseph and Mary, working in Joseph's business as a carpenter, building tables and chairs! Jesus' identity did not depend on His actions.

What we do is a *consequence* of the gifts given to us from God, but so many of us are caught in this vicious cycle of frustration and failure because we look to the things we *do* as the *source* of who we *are*. As soon as we fail in some way or disappoint others, we no longer feel good about ourselves. A poor performance shatters our confidence and we lose sight of the gifts and callings that God has revealed to us. We question our ability and then doubt the very core of who we are. Many people live for decades seeking to discover their identity but are never able to find it because they are looking in the wrong place.

This is one of the reasons why I am not into giving people titles. We had a person working for us a number of years ago in Africa. He would always call me 'Reverend' as a way of showing respect. Whenever I would say to him, "Don't call me Reverend," all he could say in response was, "Yes, Reverend." He just couldn't help himself. When I tried to tell him to treat me as his brother and friend, he would insist on calling me by a lofty title out of some false respect.

This man couldn't stop calling me "Reverend" for this reason. For him, the title had everything to do with identity. The way he saw it was if you take the title away then the identity disappears along with it. He needed that title to somehow affirm the calling on my life. It meant nothing to me; I was just happy to be my Father's son. When your identity is connected to a title, then your identity is rooted in what you do and not in who you are. It doesn't matter if you call me a prophet, a priest, an apostle, or an evangelist or just "Andy," I *know* who I am in Christ.

When I first traveled to Liberia I met a pastor who was interested in our ministry. As soon as I stepped into the hotel this man pulled me to the side and sat me down. He said, "Now, Andy Glover, I have looked at your website and all that you do and I want to know who you are. What is your title?" I wanted to reply, "I'm a man! I do a little bit of this and a little bit of that." The man's question to me again revealed that he was equating identity with activity. He wanted to identify me by the things I did instead of who I was to the Father.

If we have the eyes of the Spirit we *don't need* to ask each other questions like that. Why are we so attracted to labels and titles? If a brother or sister does something honorable, then honor is rightly due to them. However, we go overboard in rating people on the basis of who is most gifted, who can give the most prophetic words, or who has the grandest title. The reason we do this is because we ourselves are looking for identity from those things.

Keeping in mind what I have just said about identity, let me look at 2 Kings 2. This tells us about the final moments of Elijah's life on earth before he is taken up to heaven in the whirlwind. More important, however, the same scenario is the birthing moment of *Elisha's* future life and *his* entry into prophetic destiny. The narrative begins from verse 1:

"And it came to pass, when the LORD was about to take up Elijah into heaven by a whirlwind, that Elijah went with Elisha from Gilgal. Then Elijah said to Elisha, "Stay here, please, for the LORD has sent me on to Bethel." But Elisha said, "As the LORD lives, and as your soul lives, I will not leave you!" So they went down to Bethel.

Now the sons of the prophets who were at Bethel came out to Elisha, and said to him, "Do you know that the LORD will take away your master from over you today? "And he said, "Yes, I know; keep silent! Then Elijah said to him, "Elisha, stay here, please, for the LORD has sent me on to Jericho." But he said, "As the LORD lives, and as your soul lives, I will not leave you!" So they came to Jericho.

Now the sons of the prophets who were at Jericho came to Elisha and said to him, "Do you know that the LORD will take away your master from over you today? So he answered, "Yes, I know; keep silent!" Then Elijah said to him, "Stay here, please, for the LORD has sent me on to the Jordan." But he said, "As the LORD lives, and as your soul lives, I will not leave you!"

So the two of them went on. And fifty men of the sons of the prophets went and stood facing them at a distance, while the two of them stood by the Jordan. Now Elijah took his mantle, rolled it up, and struck the water; and it was divided this way and that, so that the two of them crossed over on dry ground.

— 2 KINGS 2: 1-8

Elisha had persisted in staying with his spiritual father, Elijah. Elijah then turned Elisha:

And so it was, when they had crossed over, that Elijah said to Elisha, "Ask! What may I do for you before I am taken away from you?"

— VERSE 9A

Elisha's answer is very familiar to us. It has often been preached on and widely talked about. Here is the insight I have been shown into what Elisha says:

"Please let a double portion of your spirit be upon me."

— VERSE 9B

Now, I had always thought that this *double portion* blessing was a double infilling of the Holy Spirit. But as I pondered more deeply it struck me that it just doesn't make sense to see it that way. It is impossible to fill someone twice. Admittedly, you may leak a bit and then ask the Holy Spirit to fill you afresh. However, it doesn't work either mathematically, physically, or spiritually to fill someone to the brim twice. That is an impossibility! Of course, we want as much of the Holy Spirit as possible, but that is not what this verse means. I began to discover that this double portion was *not* about the endowment of power. **It was a request for *identity.***

Elisha had followed Elijah, and he knew, beyond doubt, that there was a destiny, a call, and a purpose upon his life. As he came to these final moments in his ministry service underneath Elijah, all he wanted from Elijah was a double portion of Elijah's spirit, so he asked Elijah, *"Let a double portion of your spirit be upon me."* Elisha had one final chance to receive all the gifts and vision from Elijah that he needed to walk in his life's destiny. If he was to fulfill the mission begun through Elijah, he had to be all that he needed to be. It was time to grow up! It was time to step into his destiny and be the fullness of who God created him to be.

In order to develop my revelation about Elisha, I need to explore what this double portion of anointing actually means. The term "double portion" is not used in the New Testament, however, it *is* used a number of times in the Old Testament. One of the times it is used is in the book of Deuteronomy, where we read:

"But he shall acknowledge the son of the unloved wife as the firstborn by giving him a double portion of all that he has, for he is the beginning of his strength; the right of the firstborn is his."

— DEUTERONOMY 21:17

Elisha knew what he was asking for. Elijah knew as well. As followers of Yahweh, the words of the Hebrew Torah would have been embedded deep within their hearts. According to God's instructions given through Moses, a father was to bestow his blessing upon the firstborn son in his household prior to his death, regardless of whether this son was born of the favored mother or not. This was especially pertinent if the firstborn's mother had previously died and the father was now married to a new wife. It would have been tempting to bestow the rights of the firstborn to the firstborn son of the new wife but this was not in accordance with God's heart or justice. The true firstborn, even if he was an outcast or rejected by the living mother, would still receive the generational blessing. This blessing included a double portion of the father's possessions, both his material wealth *as well as* a spiritual inheritance. The continuation of the family heritage would continue through the firstborn's generational line.

Knowing this, we can now see the direct simplicity of Elisha's request. In essence, Elisha's request was, "Elijah, before you leave me today, I want you to bestow upon me the rights of the firstborn." In other words, "I want to be your *son*."

Elisha's request for the double portion had *nothing* to do with the endowment of power, even though that was what he received. Elisha was requesting *sonship*. He was asking to be a *son*.

Elisha knew that his calling was beyond his human capacity. He knew that he needed divine empowerment, but the only thing that he wanted was to be Elijah's son. Elisha knew that he could not embark upon a miraculous ministry of signs and wonders without receiving his full identity as a *son*. He could not guarantee his authority as a prophetic voice to the nation of Israel without first receiving the fullness of anointing that had rested upon Elijah. He *needed* to be Elijah's son. In effect, he was saying, "Elijah, I want to be your son. I want people to look at me and see *you*."

We see the same principle illustrated through Jesus. Those who questioned Jesus' authority approached Him and asked, "Jesus, who are you? Who do you think you are to perform these miracles?" Jesus would simply reply, "If you've seen me, then you have seen the Father." (John 14:8) In other words, if they looked at Jesus they could see the visible, spiritual resemblance of the Father. In character, in nature, in presence; in every sense and respect, they saw the

Father coming forth from Jesus.

Elisha's request was that Israel would see him but it was more so that they would see Elijah. Elisha would be called Elijah's son. It was that Elisha who would carry the authority and identity of Elijah, his spiritual father. All that he needed to move forward was the identity and anointing of sonship.

Sonship can only be given by a father. Sonship always derives from a father. My sons were born from my seed; they came from their father. Elisha was not the natural child of Elijah so he *requested* his sonship from Elijah. Only Elijah, the father, could grant such a request and call Elisha out into his destiny. Without Elijah's blessing the double portion anointing would never come to Elisha and he would not be able to enter into his calling.

How did Elijah respond to Elisha's request? It was a difficult request. Elisha would be his spiritual son, brought into the stream of prophetic anointing in which Elijah flowed. Elijah replied to Elisha:

> *"You have asked a hard thing. Nevertheless, if you see me when I am taken from you, it shall be so for you; but if not, it shall not be so." Then it happened, as they continued on and talked, that suddenly a chariot of fire*

*appeared with horses of fire, and separated
the two of them; and Elijah went up by a
whirlwind into heaven.*

*And Elisha saw it, and he cried out, "My
father, my father, the chariot of Israel and its
horsemen!" So he saw him no more. And he
took hold of his own clothes and tore them
into two pieces.*

— 2 KINGS 2:10-12

The double portion blessing was not about a request for power or title. Rather, it was for identity. This transfer of identity, this bestowing of inheritance and destiny is not to be taken lightly. The double portion inheritance ushered Elisha into the very same calling that was on Elijah's life. Up to that point very few could compare to Elijah!

The transfer of anointing from Elijah to Elisha contains three extremely important elements that we cannot miss: Intimacy, Identity, and Inheritance. There is a definite progression to entering into the inheritance; we see this progression working in the interactions between Elijah and Elisha. The same progression works in the relationship between God the Father and His Son, Jesus. If this progression is not followed in that specific order we will not come into our inheritance. As we work through these three steps in the transfer of inheritance, any remaining traces of our orphaned heart will disappear in the experience of being loved by the Father.

PART TWO

ENTERING INTO
SONSHIP

FORGIVENESS IS CRUCIAL

∾

What we are willing to walk away from will
not have power over us.

I finished the previous chapter by talking about three progressive steps which bring us into this double-portion anointing. However, before I go there, I need to address a very important issue.

There are very few attitudes of the heart that can separate us from complete intimacy with the Father like that of unforgiveness. Unforgiveness is a life-threatening disease that can quickly cut us off from communication with both God and man. This whole issue is a very personal work that the Holy Spirit has been doing within my own heart in recent days.

When I begin speaking on forgiveness people have different reactions. They think thoughts like these; "Now Andy looks quite mature, he has a ministry and speaks all over the world, and has been a Christian for 30 years, so why does Andy need to share about something as basic as forgiveness? Why does God need to do a work of forgiveness in *his* heart?" The truth is, God has been working in me in a deeper way than ever before in this whole area of forgiveness.

In order to come into relationship with the Father we need to come to a place of totally forgiving others for any wrong that has happened to us. This applies especially to our parents. We must release and forgive our earthly parents for any wrong we feel they have done to us in order to enjoy complete communion with our Heavenly Father. The reason for this is because, in reality, we have two fathers, a perfect one and an imperfect one. How we honor the imperfect one will determine our relationship with the perfect one.

Imagine yourself standing beneath an open sky, arms stretched wide and eyes gazing towards the heavens. Then, imagine a heavy-duty PVC pipe that connects directly from the tip of your head up into the heavens. This pipe is entirely suspended from above so it rests lightly upon you. The pipe represents your relationship with the Father; it is a vertical funnel connecting you directly to the Father. The pipe, when clear, opens up the pathway of communication and relationship with the Father. However, if any blockages clog the pipe, your ability to hear the Father becomes blocked as well.

Many things continuously attempt to clog up our connection to the Father. Things like selfishness, materialism, rebellion, or busyness will dim communication. However, unforgiveness blocks our connection to the Father more than anything else. Unforgiveness is like a blocked artery; eventually it will take your breath away and threaten your very life. Allowing unforgiveness to continue for too long can be fatal. Unforgiveness is a lethal weapon that the enemy uses to separate us from the Father. The Father sent His Son for the very purpose of forgiving and consequently gives us the opportunity to practice the same grace.

Matthew 6:14 tells us that, "…if you forgive men their trespasses, your heavenly Father will also forgive you." Jesus emphasizes the importance of forgiveness in the life of the believer. This issue cannot be easily dismissed, which is why we are confronting unforgiveness with full force right here.

The movie *Invictus* tells some of the story of Nelson Mandela. The title *Invictus* is taken from a poem of the same name, written by William Ernest Henley. The final stanza reads:

> *"It matters not how strait the gate,*
> *How charged with punishments the scroll,*
> *I am the master of my fate,*
> *I am the captain of my soul"*

That is so true! When it comes to this issue of forgiveness, we certainly are the masters of our fate and the captains of our souls. Very few political leaders have exemplified a forgiving heart in the way that Nelson Mandela did. For Mandela, it was forgiveness that brought him into his rightful destiny. Forgiveness is a crucial prerequisite for entering into our destiny as sons. Only we can make the choice to surrender our pride to the Father and releasing a spirit of forgiveness from a pure heart. When we do that, the Father performs heart surgery and unclogs our blocked arteries. In fact, He gives us an entirely new heart!

James Jordan, in his book *Sonship: a Journey into Father's Heart*, has brought out a crucial perspective on this issue of forgiveness.[5] I heartily recommend that you read his book or listen to his teaching on 'Heart Forgiveness.' I want to give a summary of what James teaches on this area of forgiving from the depths of our hearts.

James Jordan bases his teaching on a passage from Matthew 18 where Jesus tells a parable about forgiveness,

5. *Sonship: A Journey into Father's Heart*, M. James Jordan, Fatherheart Media, Taupo, 2014.

which reads like this:

> *"Then Peter came to Him and said, "Lord, how often shall my brother sin against me, and I forgive him? Up to seven times?"*
>
> *Jesus said to him, "I do not say to you, up to seven times, but up to seventy times seven. Therefore the kingdom of heaven is like a certain king who wanted to settle accounts with his servants. And when he had begun to settle accounts, one was brought to him who owed him ten thousand talents. But as he was not able to pay, his master commanded that he be sold, with his wife and children and all that he had, and that payment be made. The servant therefore fell down before him, saying, 'Master, have patience with me, and I will pay you all.' Then the master of that servant was moved with compassion, released him, and forgave him the debt.*
>
> *"But that servant went out and found one of his fellow servants who owed him a hundred denarii; and he laid hands on him and took him by the throat, saying, 'Pay me what you owe!' So his fellow servant fell down at his feet and begged him, saying, 'Have patience with*

me, and I will pay you all. And he would not, but went and threw him into prison till he should pay the debt. So when his fellow servants saw what had been done, they were very grieved, and came and told their master all that had been done. Then his master, after he had called him, said to him, 'You wicked servant! I forgave you all that debt because you begged me. Should you not also have had compassion on your fellow servant, just as I had pity on you?' And his master was angry, and delivered him to the torturers until he should pay all that was due to him.

"So My heavenly Father also will do to you if each of you, from his heart, does not forgive his brother his trespasses."

— MATTHEW 18:1-35

From this passage, James Jordan has drawn out a number of crucial truths:

1. Forgiveness is more than an issue of choice – it is an issue of the heart.

Many of us have been taught on multiple occasions that we must make a choice to forgive. Choosing is part of the process but you cannot simply choose with your mind that you will forgive another. You cannot just repeat a few words of a guided prayer and suddenly enjoy full restoration and reconciliation where there has been deep heartache, anger or resentment. Just as you cannot receive salvation through logical understanding, you cannot come to true forgiveness by an act of will. Salvation and forgiveness happen directly to your heart through faith.

Ask yourself this question: What is your heart willing to do? Are you willing to lay down your pride, your "right to be right," and your personal comfort for the sake of reconciliation? Do you just know that you *should* forgive or is your heart responding to the conviction of the Holy Spirit? Do you yearn for unity for the sake of the purity of the gospel? True forgiveness can only occur if it has moved from head to heart. Unforgiveness is a disease of the heart, so your heart is where the surgery must occur.

2. We must love to forgive.

Jesus took the conventional understanding of what it means to forgive and turned it on its head. Peter came to Jesus saying, "Hey Jesus, my brother is messing me around. Should I just forgive him seven times?" Jesus' reply to Peter is, "No! You must forgive him *seventy times seven*." That's 490 times!

Jesus was not trying to set a new numerical standard for

forgiveness. Rather, He was explaining to us that forgiveness is actually endless. He was showing us where our heart
must be in the matter. Forgiveness should be an endless
attitude of our hearts, becoming an enmeshed aspect of
who we are as children of God. Forgiveness must become
part of our lifestyle. The reason is because we will *always* be
placed in situations where we need to forgive.

Jesus begins His teaching on forgiveness by showing us
that it is essential to *love to forgive*. We must make forgiveness an endless pursuit that we never tire of. While Jesus
was on the cross, after being abused and violated in every
way possible, He still called out, "Father, forgive them"
(Luke 23:24). Forgiveness was part of who Jesus was and
something that He loved to do.

This is something the Father is really working on in my
heart. We can line up all the wrongs and injustices that
have been done to us, and think about all the pain, but
then the Father comes to us and says, "Ok, let go of those
things. Relinquish the right you think you have to judge
those people and walk in the freeing grace of God."

3. Forgiveness starts with an understanding of what was stolen and canceling the debt.

I love to hear Gunilla tell her story about how she forgave
her own father. Gunilla was just 13 years of age when her

mother died, it was a very traumatic time for her, as well as for her brother and her father. She had been very close to her mom and has very happy memories of her early years. After her mom's death her relationship with her father became very strained. She lived under a cloud of fear and tension every time he would come home from work. Her dad had no one to help him with the grief that he was trying to deal with. Gunilla ceased trusting her dad and did her best to stay out of his way. It became clear to Gunilla that part of her journey in forgiving her dad was to acknowledge what was stolen; her confidence, feeling safe, secure and at home, receiving encouragement, support and help with decisions. This was a revelation to her and brought her to the place of forgiving from the heart. It is important to know that forgiveness does not take away the memory, but restores our hearts.

Justice demands that the sinner make and pay full restitution. However, forgiveness lets go of what was stolen. Whether the issue is physical, financial, or emotional, forgiveness means that you let go what was stolen from you. When the master forgave the servant his debt of ten thousand talents, he was letting go of a lot of money.

I have experienced this personally. Someone took a large amount of money from me and every fiber of my being wanted to claim an injustice and be angry. Then God said to me, "Andy, just love them. Forgive them and release them." I thought to myself, "That's a great idea, God, but You know that we *need* the money!" However, through the grace of God, I was able to call this person and say to them, "I release you from this injustice of taking what you knew was mine." I was able to do that because I had released what I thought I had a right to hold onto. It took a process in my heart for me to be able to do it, a process that the Father desires to carry each of us through. He wants to set us free from the burden of clinging to what we think belongs to us.

Here is the crucial point. When we truly understand what was stolen from us then we can understand what it means to *cancel the debt*. Forgiveness has a lot to do with knowing what has been stolen from us. When we know what was taken from us, then we know what debt to cancel. That's the picture of forgiveness that Jesus talks about in Matthew 18.

4. Forgiveness is founded on a heart of compassion.

When the servant came back to his master the first time around he begged his master for mercy. The Bible tells us that the master then had compassion on him and released him from the debt (Matthew 18:27).

We will never really understand what it means to forgive unless we have some of the Father's heart for that person who has hurt and violated us. In other words, our hearts must be moved to compassion for that person. Once the master's heart was moved by compassion for the servant he was able to cancel the debt. The same is true for us. When our hearts are moved to compassion, we are able to cancel the debts of others.

I am fully aware that many of us have experienced very difficult or traumatic upbringings. I was born in 1959 and grew up in a culture in Britain where we were just getting over World War II. Many people who had served in the armed forces had returned with all sorts of horrific experiences. Often these soldiers had little emotional capacity to give love to their families. Straight away distance was created between father and son, or between father and daughter. Many children grew up with a profound sense of injustice because of the way their father was, but they never understood what their fathers endured.

The Holy Spirit is beginning to give me His compassion for my own parents. I am starting to see life from their perspective, to have insight into the struggles that they faced. Instead of judging them and being angry with them for the way I have been treated, I am receiving God's compassion for them.

When we catch Daddy's heart for someone who has hurt us, we are well on the way to forgiving them from our heart, because we have picked up what Father God feels. When we merely forgive as a decision of the will, we negate the opportunity to *feel* what the Father *feels* and know what the Father thinks. The amazing thing about Jesus is that He stepped out of His world and into our world; He identified with us. Hebrews 4:15 tells us:

> *"...we do not have a High Priest who cannot sympathize with our weaknesses, but was in all points tempted as we are, yet without sin."*

Then in Philippians 2:5, Paul writes:

> *"Let this mind be in you, which was also in Christ Jesus."*

God came and incarnated Himself, living under the same pressures and temptations that we live under. Jesus was unjustly treated, violated, and spat at. This Jesus, whom we worship, lived a life in which He forgave those who crucified Him. He is not asking us to do something that He has not already done. We can say flippantly that we want to be like Jesus but this is a vital part of it. Living a life modeled after Jesus means that we live a life consumed by a heart of compassionate forgiveness. We need to ask the Father to give us His compassion for those who have hurt us. We will be surprised to see what happens.

One of the greatest stories I have heard about forgiving

with Christ's forgiveness is that of Corrie ten Boom. Corrie and her family were held in a Nazi concentration camp during the Second World War. During her time in the concentration camp she lost both her father and her sister. Years later, she met one of the prison guards that had tortured and humiliated her and her family. Here is an excerpt from her book *The Hiding Place*.

> *"It was at a church service in Munich that I saw him, the former SS man who had stood guard at the shower room door in the processing centre at Ravensbruck. He was the first of our actual jailers that I had seen since that time. And suddenly it was all there – the roomful of mocking men, the heaps of clothing, Betsie's pain blanched face. He came up to me as the church was emptying, beaming and bowing. "How grateful I am for your message Fräulein", he said "To think that, as you say, He has washed my sins away!" His hand was thrust out to shake mine. And I, who had preached so often to the people in Bloemendaal the need to forgive, kept my hand at my side. Even as the angry, vengeful thoughts boiled through me, I saw the sin of them. Jesus Christ had died for this man; was I going to ask for more? Lord Jesus, I prayed, forgive me and help me to forgive him. I tried*

to smile, I struggled to raise my hand. I could not. I felt nothing, not the slightest spark of warmth or charity. And so again I breathed a silent prayer. Jesus, I cannot forgive him. Give me Your Forgiveness. As I took his hand the most incredible thing happened. From my shoulder along my arm and through my hand a current seemed to pass from me to him, while into my heart sprang a love for this stranger that almost overwhelmed me. And so I discovered that it is not on our forgiveness any more than on our goodness that the world's healing hinges, but on His.[6]

5. Forgiveness is relinquishing our right to judge.

When we relinquish our right to judge, the enemy loses his right to keep us trapped in bondage. As well as that, Satan loses his right to keep the other person trapped in bondage. When I forgave my dad fully, it seemed as if a fresh grace seemed to rest on his life as well as mine. Jesus told us, in John 20:23, that if we forgive the sins of anyone, then they will be forgiven As a consequence, our decision to forgive or not to forgive affects the other person's heart too. As we are obedient to forgive others, fresh grace falls on their life as well as ours.

---

6. *The Hiding Place*, Corrie Ten Boom with John and Elizabeth Sherrill, Bantam Books, New Jersey, 1971.

One of the reasons I believe that our families are not getting saved is because we are still holding our parents, our siblings, and our other relatives in judgment. Once we forgive, we release a fresh grace over the generations.

Romans 2:1 tells us:

> *"Therefore you have no excuse, or defense, or justification, O man, whoever you are who condemns and judges another. For in posing as judge and passing sentence on another, you condemn yourself, because you who judge are habitually practicing the very same things [that you censure and denounce.]"*
>
> — AMPLIFIED BIBLE

We become the very thing that we judge! I have seen this played out in my life and the lives of others time and time again.

6. *The torture of unforgiveness is the holding on to that which was already taken.*

When you do not forgive, your heart becomes calloused. Every time you think about the perpetrator and that crime against you, it runs like a repeating video in your mind. The injustice is magnified in your mind more than it ever was to begin with. When we hold on to this injustice we suffer constant torture from a burden that we cannot escape from. The pain that we choose to hold on to affects us emotionally and spiritually, Eventually, it also affects us physically. Some sicknesses are rooted in an unwillingness to let go of pain and unforgiveness.

There have been a number of times in my life when I have harbored unforgiveness in my heart in relation to different individuals. These people have then become prominent in my thinking and feelings, and have ultimately influenced my decision making. I can't get them off my mind and when their names are brought up all the negative thoughts and emotions rise to the surface. My heart starts to suffer and I go through an emotional torture. Thankfully the Father has always given me the grace to forgive from the heart, which releases my heart and mind from unnecessary festering of pain. My heart reactions to people has been an honest indicator of what I need to let go of. It took us a long time to fully forgive our former leader in Ghana, but today my heart reaches out to him in compassion.

When your heart is connected to someone in unforgiveness, then it is not free to fully connect to your heavenly Father. In other words, if you are still connected through unforgiveness to your parents, and if you are holding judgement in your heart, that part of your heart cannot possibly connect to your heavenly Daddy. Often, that is the reason for your disconnect in your relationship with God.

People often come to me in counseling and say, "I don't know what's wrong with me! I can't connect with God. I can't feel the Holy Spirit." I often respond, "Oh, it's very simple. You just need to deal with some of these issues in your heart." They are more connected to who has hurt them than to God.

I don't know about you, but I don't want anything to get in the way of my connection to my heavenly Father. Right now, as you are processing through all that I have shared with you, I invite you to take a moment and ask the Father to reveal to you any person or any injustice that you are still clinging to. Is there anything or anyone to which you have not fully extended forgiveness? If so, you will not be able to fully grasp a revelation of the Father's love for you. If you are still burdened by the pain of unforgiveness in regard to your earthly parents, you will not be able to inherit all that He has for you as a son or daughter.

Some of us also need to forgive ourselves. We need to forgive ourselves for the mistakes we have made and release ourselves from our own judgments. The Father offers that forgiveness today.

Having established the absolute need to come to a place of true forgiveness, let me return to talking about the three spiritual elements involved in coming into the inheritance of sonship.

As I have studied the relationship between Elijah and Elisha in 2 Kings 2, the Holy Spirit has opened my eyes to see a recurring pattern throughout Scripture. Whenever we see an interaction between a father and a son, or whenever a son or daughter is being birthed into his (or her) purposes for the Kingdom, these three elements always occur.

The three factors in the call to sonship are ***intimacy***, ***identity***, and ***inheritance*** (or destiny).

They work in that order and cannot be rearranged. Wherever a call into sonship occurs in Scripture, whether in the Old Testament or the New Testament, the same sequence applies. Over the next three chapters I want to look at these three elements in detail.

CHAPTER FIVE

INTIMACY: REMOVING THE CLOAK OF SHAME

~

Shame hides the fearful heart in an illusion that our Father is angry and disapproves of our lives, we revert to law to satisfy the demands of an angry God. Grace, however, is found in vulnerability and unlocks all the treasures of the Father's love.

The first element in coming into the inheritance of sonship is *intimacy*. Whenever I describe *intimacy*, I explain that intimacy means 'in-to-me-see.' The dictionary says that intimacy is a "close familiarity." An intimate encounter with the Father is essential for us to develop a deep, meaningful relationship and familiarity in our walk with Him. Intimacy loses its intrinsic beauty when we hide behind shame, fear and control. Intimacy has coincided with God's design for relationship since the creation of man in the Garden of Eden. However, like Adam, many are never fully able to embrace an intimate relationship with the Father. Many people never let the Father into the depths of who they are. As a result, most Christians never reach the fullness of their purpose in the Kingdom.

If we go back to the story of Elijah and Elisha, we see that Elisha was about to be birthed into the very calling that was on Elijah's life. In that story, we find an unexpected, intimate encounter. After Elisha made his request for a double portion of Elijah's spirit, Elijah affirmed that if Elisha saw him as he was taken up, then he (Elisha) would have his request granted. So, the chariot came down and Elijah was caught up in the whirlwind. When he saw that, Elisha cried out, *"My father my father!"* Elisha was determined not to lose sight of Elijah because he knew that Elijah had the ability to bestow true identity into his heart.

Elisha *pursued* Elijah. Elisha shamelessly pursued Elijah, not willing for him to leave until he (Elisha) would receive the strength and authority needed to continue Elijah's ministry. Where intimacy is desired, a pursuit *must* occur.

This was the case in my life. As the Father was coming close to my heart a number of years ago, I experienced Him pursuing me. He encouraged me to take six months off from the hectic schedule of ministry and just sit in a chair and listen to worship music; a spiritual discipline called "soaking." I needed intimacy with the Father so that I could grow into the person He had really called me to be. The Father needed me to let my guard down and allow Him to love me. Not only was the Father pursuing my heart, but it was my responsibility to let my heart be pursued. I had to keep my focus on Him, allowing myself to be vulnerable to the Father's intimate love. For a "Type A" personality like me, it was one of the hardest things I have ever had to do.

It is absolutely wonderful to realize that we are being pursued by God. When we know we are being pursued, the wisest thing we can do is surrender to it. Elisha was determined to stay with Elijah because of what Elijah was about to do. Elisha knew that the only way to receive and begin to walk in his destiny was to have a pivotal encounter with Elijah. He had to pursue his spiritual father until the end. He was shameless, vulnerable, and fully dedicated in his quest to know and to become all that Elijah was.

Why did Elisha need to pursue Elijah? Why did he cry out "My father, my father!" with the desperation of a young child? Why was it so important for Elisha to ask and seek his father, Elijah, for the blessings? The reason is that sonship can only be bestowed by a *father*.

In nature, it is the father who can reproduce his seed; the same is true in the spiritual life. In Jewish culture, sons are bestowed a blessing from their father at the Bar Mitzvah ceremony. Why? Because sonship derives from the father. The seed of sonship exists with the father.

The problem today is that many are uncomfortable with this idea of intimacy. Some have experienced immense pain when it comes to their relationship with their earthly fathers, therefore the idea of intimacy with a heavenly Father seems entirely foreign, if not outright intimidating. Perhaps this entire concept of fathers and sonship is slipping right through *your* fingers. Are you missing out on intimacy with your heavenly Father?

Many are searching and seeking for intimacy in all the wrong places, only to miss the one source of intimacy they need most; an encounter with God the Father. They search for love and acceptance from frivolous sexual encounters or from a host of so-called friends, only to find themselves more alone and dejected than before. Soon an orphan spirit emerges within their hearts. As these fatherless children grow and reproduce, the orphan spirit they carry is reproduced in turn. Orphans reproduce orphans. Only fathers can reproduce sons.

What did Elisha do when he saw Elijah caught up into the whirlwind? In 2 Kings 2:12 we read:

> *"And Elisha saw it, and he cried out, "My*
> *father, my father, the chariot of Israel and its*
> *horsemen!" So he saw him no more. And he*
> *took hold of his own clothes and tore them*
> *into two pieces."*

Elijah is in the middle of being taken up, and there we find Elisha undressing! Off comes his cloak! Elisha is literally tearing his clothes off! Isn't that an odd picture to pop into your mind while reading the Bible? Can you *get any* more vulnerable and shameless? The desperation for his father had reached the breaking point and there was no longer anything to hide. The ability for true intimacy to occur was finally made real.

I want us to see another encounter in Scripture where this call for intimacy, this call for an unabridged and intimate relationship with the Father, is seen. Here, we see another prophetic allegorical picture that God must intimately connect with our hearts in order for sonship to be bestowed.

In Genesis 3, we read about the first man and woman to walk the earth, Adam and Eve. Adam and Eve were created and destined for perfect communion with the Father. They were naked, living completely shameless and intimate lives with God and one another. But, then the great sin occurred. As a result of the lie of the serpent's tongue, they forgot who they were and became blinded to their sonship, Suddenly, guilt and shame crept into the depths of Adam and Eve's souls, and in Genesis 3:7 we read,

> *"Then the eyes of both of them were opened, and they knew that they were naked; and they sewed fig leaves together and made themselves coverings."*

Why did they do that? How could they have lived for decades without one fiber of cloth covering their bodies and now they are running about in a nervous frenzy looking for a needle and thread? The reason is that they had now sinned. As a result, they concluded that they were bad people destined for judgment, and now they needed to protect themselves. They didn't feel good about who they were anymore. In fact, they ran from who they were, hiding in the bushes from the very One who had known them more closely than any other; the One who created them from His very breath—their Father, God.

It is essential that God deals with our shame. Shame manifests itself throughout our lives, bringing emotionally charged feelings of guilt and insecurity that can literally bind our hearts in chains. Shame lies to us about the very essence of our identity and value. God wants to get to the depths of our spirit and reveal to us who we *really* are so that we can live out of that. Our shame has covered us with an impenetrable shroud over our spirits that prevents us from intimate relationship with the Father.

When I look back over my own life, the mightiest stronghold that I have had to uncover is *shame*. I am so thankful for over thirty hours of ministry from *Restoring the Foundations* ministry that uncovered my shameful heart. False identity had covered my heart for many years. I was buried beneath layers of shame and guilt that left me believing I could never be loved for who I truly was. It was the assurance that I was loved by the Father, simply because I was His child, and the revelation that I was fully accepted into His family, that set me free. I pray that God grants you the same revelation, no matter what may be contributing to the shame and guilt operating within your heart.

Sin affects every part of who we are. Our spirits, souls and bodies are all interconnected and are simultaneously affected by sin. When we sin we become ashamed of the way God has made us. We loathe ourselves, seeking any means and methods to try to cover ourselves up. We subconsciously think, "I don't like the way I look to God right now so I will make some fig leaves for myself and cover up! He won't notice the difference, right?" Life then becomes an issue of controlling our environment and fearing the Lord God walking in the garden. God wants to get right to the depths of our hearts, and He cannot do that if we are constantly hiding from Him in shame.

When it comes to living how God has called us to be, fear and shame are the most dangerous disablers of our hearts. Shame plants deception into the core of our hearts, causing us to hide from God, swamped by feelings of unworthiness and hopelessness. The intensity of shame we feel is so unbearable that many of us, like Adam and Eve, would rather lie to ourselves and others than face the realities of our sin. We believe that we have caused God huge disappointment and we fear the consequences.

This is exactly what Adam and Eve did when facing the reality of their sin. In Genesis 3:8 we read:

> *"And they heard the sound of the LORD God walking in the garden in the cool of the day, and Adam and his wife hid themselves from the presence of the LORD God among the trees of the garden. Then the LORD God called to Adam and said to him, "Where are you?" So he said, "I heard your voice in the garden, and I was afraid because I was naked; and I hid myself."*

How is it that the God of all creation, who is truly omnipresent, appeared to give the impression that He could not find Adam and Eve in the garden? How could an omnipresent and omniscient God lose them? The truth is, He hadn't really lost them; He knew *exactly* where they were.

God was not confused about the physical location of Adam, but His question, "Adam, where are you?" had everything to do with the fact that Adam was now hiding his *heart* from God. Adam was ashamed of what he had done and, like a little child, he was hiding under his bed hoping his daddy wouldn't find him. The fig leaves that Adam and Eve covered themselves with were a symbol of what was going on in their hearts. In their hearts they were hiding from the presence of the Father.

Shame hides the fearful heart in response to an illusion that our Father is angry and disapproves of our lives. We then revert to the law to satisfy the demands of what we perceive to be an angry God. Grace, however, is found in vulnerability and unlocks all the treasures of the Father's love.

It is easy to confess our sin, but getting over the residual guilt and shame of that sin is an entirely different affair. Adam and Eve knew that God saw what they had done but they could not face the guilt and shame within their own hearts. Then the Father came to Adam and said, "Hello, where are you? I know where you are physically, Adam, but how do I get into your heart?" Father God wasn't there to chastise them; He was pursuing their hearts. The intimacy they enjoyed with Father God had been broken.

God's discipline does not derive from a foundation of guilt. His discipline is meant to show us the loving way out of our predicament while maintaining a loving relationship with us. When we are so influenced by this negative impression of ourselves, however, we develop a negative impression of who *God* is. We do not believe that God is a Father of unconditional love and forgiveness. In our faulty beliefs, we block the very road to freedom. We hide ourselves from true intimacy with the Father, thereby rejecting God's loving pursuit. We are fearful and turn to legalism to satisfy the demands of an 'angry' God.

How does all this connect with Elijah and Elisha? As Elijah was taken into heaven and his mantle was falling, Elisha's reaction is to tear off his clothes. The mantle is symbolic of his identity being connected with Elijah. As a response, he *makes himself* naked. It is unlikely that anyone witnessed this but it shows the attitude of Elisha's heart. Elisha strips himself naked, one of the most intimate and shameless of all actions imaginable. He does so in preparation for the double portion coming to him. He expects the blessing, the identity, the purpose to fall upon him, and he is completely and utterly open.

Adam covered himself in shame, moved away from his sonship and closed his heart. In contrast, Elisha tore off his cloak, *entered into sonship*, and *opened* his heart to the future destined for him. What Elisha did was the opposite of what Adam did. It was a reversal of what happened in the garden.

If we are ever going to receive our identity and inherit our prophetic destiny, we need to come to that same level of openness and vulnerability before Father God. We must bare all in complete surrender, completely transparent before Him. Our heart must cry out, "Now, You are coming and I am rendering myself naked before You, because You want to get into the very depths of my being!"

Recently, the Father spoke to me twice, once through a dream and once through a vision. The dream was so prophetic that I was unsure what realm I was in when I woke up. I had the dream in Sweden where my family and I now have our home. In the dream, I was in the upstairs bedroom of a large Victorian house. There were four colossal windows through which I could see a massive storm cloud approaching. The wind began howling throughout the house, rattling the window panes. As the storm drew closer, the window panes shook harder and harder until they shattered into multiple tiny shards of glass across the bedroom. Suddenly, the storm was inside the house! I stood in utter amazement at this powerful torrent of creation. There was nothing I could do to defend or protect myself. As I considered the dream, I asked the Lord to reveal to me what it was about. God then showed me that He was speaking to me about what He wanted to do with me individually and with His Church. God wants to break into the boundaries of our hearts and burst into our lives.

As I was meditating about my dream, I had a vision. I found myself wandering among the hills of Sweden when, again, a storm suddenly broke out. Howling wind and rain, flashing lightning and booming thunder battered me as I stood in the midst of this storm. I was dressed up in a heavy coat like those worn in the Swedish winters.

The wind became so strong that it began to rip off portions of my clothes. With all my might, I attempted to salvage what clothing I still had, but no matter how hard I tried I could not succeed. The storm moved on, leaving me naked and vulnerable.

As I was experiencing this vision and asking God what it meant, He began to show me that He is pursuing the core of our hearts. We always want to see the power of God in revival but *He* is going for our hearts. If we experience a move of the Holy Spirit but don't allow the Holy Spirit into our hearts, we will never really get what He is trying to do in us or in His Church. We will miss out on the full glory and blessing.

Oftentimes, we can have dynamic worship music with penetrating lyrics yet miss the intimate presence of Father God. The Holy Spirit is going for the very core of our hearts. He has to gust in with His presence and strip us bare in order to penetrate to the core of who we are. God is contending for something that we have not always been willing to give. He is willing to strip us down, shed our clothes, and break the glass to get to the core of our being. Without stripping us naked, rendering us vulnerable, and encountering us in an intimate way, His presence will only touch the surface. Father God is willing to strip things off us in order to get to the root of who we are. Until He does so, we can never experience the intimacy required to become His true sons and daughters.

In order for identity to be bestowed, there has to be an encounter of intimacy on the inside of our hearts. The seed of reproduction is released in intimacy and the seed carries on to formulate an identity. As soon as my father's seed entered my mother's womb, there was the identity of Andrew John Glover.

The same is true spiritually. The incredible thing is that we had an identity in God before the creation of the world. Then God gives us a destiny that is directly connected with our identity. Before the creation of the world we were in the heart of the Father. Isn't that amazing?

CHAPTER SIX

IDENTITY: SPIRITUAL SONSHIP

~

Sonship lies at the heart of the Father's redemptive plan for our lives.

The second element in coming into the inheritance of sonship is *identity*. Intimacy always precedes identity. If we want to come into our inheritance, we can only do so as sons and daughters. The term *sonship* is an identity statement. You are a son to the Father, living in a revelation of the Father's love and the Father's authority, bearing His image in anticipation of one day receiving His inheritance. It is fundamental that we understand that God is a loving Father. Many believers know *about* the Father but they have no experiential revelation of His love.

Orphans never receive an inheritance because they do not know what it is to have a father. For many years I believed that my sonship was connected to my performance or my ability to behave in a certain way. My view was similar to that of the lost son who intended to say to his father, "…make me like one of your hired servants" (Luke 15:19). In my heart I had not caught the real meaning of redemption, for the very simple reason that I had not encountered the Father. It was for this purpose that I was saved, that I may be redeemed back to the Father, not as an adopted child or a servant, *but as a son*. We were created as His, conceived in His heart before the foundation of the world (Ephesians 1:4), and our redemption is simply our journey back to our source, the Father.

For many years I looked to my ministry as the source of my identity. I was constantly striving to serve others while, back at home, my wife Gunilla struggled daily with my attitude and behavior. My emotions would fluctuate dramatically in tandem with how well the ministry seemed to be going. It was as though ministry was my only source of affirmation. There was a continual identity crisis going on in my heart and mind.

Because we do not know to whom we belong, we do not know who we really are. As the Father's love started to pour into my heart, it was then that I started to discover who I really was; I was a *son*. From that time on, the Father has done a wonderful work of restoration within my family.

This is true for all of us. We were spiritual orphans, destined for a future devoid of hope and blessing. The Father extended His hand of gracious love, inviting us back into His eternal family. He offers us a way back into sonship through the redemptive work of Jesus (2 Corinthians 5:18). He gives us an identity that we could never attain outside of His invitation. Sonship can only be bestowed by a Father; it is the seed of the Father's intimacy that bears a son. There is nothing we can do on our own to prove our worthiness to be a son. It is part of the Father's redemptive work, drawing us back to the place of our true identity as sons and daughters.

Now, let's go a bit further with this concept of *identity*. Before we consider it in the relationship between Elijah and Elisha, let us turn to the eighth chapter of Romans. In this chapter, I want to identify three points of recognition that are crucial to our understanding of identity. When identity as a son is bestowed, we will realize these three things regarding the Father's love.

Firstly, that we are ***beloved***;
Secondly, that we ***belong***;
Thirdly, that we are ***blessed***.

These are the three 'Bs' of spiritual identity: *Beloved, Belong, and Blessed*. I am His beloved, I belong to Him and

I am blessed. When those three truths are established in your heart, everything is resolved. There is no longer any shame, fear, guilt or worry. There is no more orphan spirit.

Romans 8:15 says:

> *"For you did not receive the spirit of bondage*
> *again to fear, but you received the Spirit of*
> *adoption by whom we cry out, "Abba, Father."*

Here, in Romans 8, we see that the seed of the Father, the bestowing of identity, comes into our hearts with the presence of the Holy Spirit. When the Holy Spirit of sonship comes into us the most natural thing that follows is to cry, "Abba Daddy, You are here. I worship you and acknowledge you!" We recognize that we are His beloved, that we belong to Him and that we are blessed for all eternity. This is where identity is formulated.

This understanding that the identity of sons is based on being beloved, belonging, and being blessed is illustrated beautifully in Luke 15. There we read the parable known as 'The Prodigal Son.' This is one of the most striking displays of a father's love throughout the entire Scripture. As I meditated on this passage, the Holy Spirit revealed to me again what I have already been emphasizing throughout this book. There is a progression from intimacy to identity, and then from identity to inheritance.

In the parable in Luke 15, the younger son requests his portion of his inheritance while his father is still living. He leaves the father's house and squanders his inheritance on prostitutes, alcohol, and other fleshly indulgences. Then the son finds an empty money bag on his belt and is unable to secure for himself another meal. He searches for a job for survival, and ultimately finds himself eating among the pigs, which are the most unclean of all animals in the Jewish culture. He is lonely, destitute, and hopeless. He is an orphan in need of a father.

Then the son comes up with a bright idea to return home. He decides to beg his father to let him serve as a hired hand on his estate. The prodigal son is trying to *earn* his way back into the family by what he can *do*. He doesn't know who he is anymore; he has lost his identity as his father's son. Destitute and hungry, he makes his way back home:

> *"But when he was still a great way off, his father saw him and had compassion, and ran and fell on his neck and kissed him. And the son said to him, 'Father, I have sinned against heaven and in your sight, and am no longer worthy to be called your son.'"*
>
> — LUKE 15:20,21

What does his father do? He sees his son in the distance and he *runs* towards him. He jumps on him, kisses him, and embraces him. This daddy is a radical lover, even towards a son that has shamed, stolen from, and deserted him. You see, the term 'prodigal' is translated to mean something extreme or over the top. The term 'prodigal' not only refers to sinful behavior, but also to *loving* and *righteous* behavior. This father is *also* a prodigal! He does not hold his love back. He is so radically in love with his son that he exhibits it through a *prodigal* display of intimate affection towards his undeserving and apprehensive son.

There are three primary ways by which humans communicate love towards one another. Through the eyes (what we see), the ears (what we hear), and touch (what we feel). All of these ways of communicating love are displayed in this passage. In the reinstatement of the son to his father, the son *sees* the father running, *feels* his intimate embrace, and *hears* words of profound forgiveness and grace. The prodigal son knew that he was fully loved!

In verses 22-24 we read:

> *"But the father said to his servants, 'Bring out the best robe and put it on him, and put a ring on his hand and sandals on his feet. And bring the fatted calf here and kill it, and let us eat and be merry; for this my son was dead and is alive again; he was lost and is found.' And they began to be merry."*

What love, what acceptance, and what blessing this father bestowed! There were no requests for an apology, no guilt-ridden lecture that the son was forced to endure. There was only pure and unrestrained mercy and love. Who do you think owned the best robe? Whose ring was placed on the son's finger? It was the *father's* robe and the *father's* ring! The father was, in essence, communicating full acceptance back into the family, and he let everyone in the land know it. What a moving illustration of what the Father does for us, His children! The Father clothes us with heavenly garments and places His identifying ring upon our finger. Hallelujah!

This son had done nothing to deserve this stretch of extravagant mercy and grace. In fact, he had done everything to deserve rejection, judgment, and a future racked with desolation and shame. In requesting his inheritance early the son was essentially declaring that he wished his father was dead. According to Mosaic law, the father had every right to take his son to the court and accuse him of a crime. In fact, Exodus 21:17 states that anyone who cursed his father was to be punished by death! The curse of this son towards his father was the ultimate expression of dishonor and a direct violation of God's commandment to honor one's father and mother (Exodus 20:12). This underlines, even more so, the graciousness and love of this father towards his son.

The inheritance is only given to sons; only fathers can bestow sonship. This father, in Luke 15, loved his son, identified his son, and restored the destiny of blessing to his son. This son was beloved, he belonged, and he was blessed.

There is one final point about Luke 15 that I want to make. The son in this parable had to make a choice. He could either receive his father's affection with humility and thankfulness or he could decide not to. What if the son had come back after his father's display of merciful love and said, "Oh no father! I cannot receive this. I'm too unworthy. I must work to somehow earn my way back into your household. Otherwise, I will never be able to live with myself again?" You see, the son had to open up his heart to receive his father's love and his identity as his son. He had to yield his pride in exchange for the humility required to receive an undeserved blessing. He had to overcome the shame that held him in bondage and believe that he could be loved again.

The same is true for us. Our Father runs towards us with extended arms, yearning to cover us with His love and identify us as His sons and daughters. He has blessings waiting specifically for us, and a future inheritance unlike any known to the earth. Like the son in this parable, we have the choice as to whether we will receive the Father's identity or not. Will we believe that we are beloved, that we able to belong, and that we are blessed? We must receive the spirit of sonship, we must be placed as sons and daughters (Romans 8:15), if we are to receive the inheritance that goes with it. Sonship derives from our encounter with the Father because the origin of the Spirit of sonship comes from the Father.

In the story of Elijah and Elisha, we see Elijah taken up into heaven and Elisha naked crying out, "My father, my father!" Then, we read:

> *"He (Elisha) also took up the mantle of Elijah that had fallen from him, and went back and stood by the bank of the Jordan. Then he took the mantle of Elijah that had fallen from him, and struck the water, and said, "Where is the LORD God of Elijah?" And when he also had struck the water, it was divided this way and that; and Elisha crossed over.*
>
> *Now when the sons of the prophets who were from Jericho saw him, they said, "The spirit of Elijah rests on Elisha." And they came to meet him, and bowed to the ground before him."*
>
> — 2 KINGS 2:13-15

I love this. Elisha comes out of this encounter with Elijah and he rolls up the same cloak that Elijah had been wearing. Then, he strikes the water and the water divides just as it had done for Elijah (2 Kings 2:8). The sons of the prophets are watching and they say to him, "...the Spirit and power that was on Elijah is on Elisha." It is amazing! Identity has been bestowed. Elisha's request for sonship has been granted. When they look at Elisha, they see Elijah. All of Elijah's prophetic anointing and miraculous power now rests upon his son, Elisha.

Jesus said, "If you have seen me, you have seen the Father" (John 14:7). The same is true for us. When we receive our identity as a son or daughter from the Father, then others see the Father in us. As sons, we are able to carry the very image of an invisible Father God to a world full of orphans who need to encounter His love.

When we walk in sonship, we live in a fresh authority, a fresh favor and, most of all, a fresh realization that Daddy is very close. The struggle to strive and manipulate is no longer part of our agenda. Rather, our desire to reveal a loving Father is the driving force of our life. Our life becomes a pursuit of the *Father's* mission. That is because the Elijah Spirit always wants to father, the Elijah Spirit always wants to bring the prophetic mantle and the Elijah Spirit always wants to see things restored. The Elijah Spirit is a spirit of sonship destined for your heart and with it comes an indescribable destiny.

CHAPTER SEVEN

INHERITANCE: WALKING INTO DESTINY

∼

Inheritance is being at home with our Father and fully allowing Him to live His purpose through our lives.

If the first two elements in sonship are intimacy and identity, in that specific order, then the third element is **inheritance**. Another term for 'inheritance' is 'destiny.'

Inheritance only comes and goes to sons. Why is this so important? All that I have shared across the nations about receiving a revelation of the Father's love is bound together by this 'pinnacle principle.' If you do not understand that you must be a son or daughter of the Father in order to walk in His full blessing and inheritance, then you hold an incomplete understanding of the extent to which God desires to be in relationship with us.

We all want the inheritance. We all want to know our *destiny,* our purpose for existence here on earth. Our culture is full of people who are infatuated with discovering why they were created and how their unique purpose differentiates them from everyone else. Parents teach it, schools teach it, and churches teach it. What is your purpose? What is your destiny? Nothing can trigger stress, discouragement, or doubt like a Christian who cannot grasp his or her spiritual destiny. Many stand paralyzed in the work of the Kingdom, unable to move forward without knowing which direction to move.

The problem with all of this destiny-seeking is that it stems from a mentality that is still bound to the approval of men. We want to know *what* we are supposed to be *doing* rather than *who* we are supposed to *be*. Our seeking of destiny is based on a belief that we have to *do* something, instead of living out of who we already are. We bombard God with questions such as, "Where am I supposed to be serving? What job or ministry am I supposed to pursue? To what nations are You calling me to preach the Gospel?" These are all valid questions in themselves, but they derive from a heart still seeking to earn acceptance and approval from the Father through *doing*. We are so concerned that if we somehow miss this definitive purpose on our lives then we are going to miss the Father. We will miss our inheritance. We are living in fear, bound to the earth rather than walking and resting in the Spirit.

If you can see into the spiritual reality, then the answer you are looking for will become clear. Your purpose and my purpose is to live as a son, or daughter, of our Father God. This was precisely why Adam was created, and it is why the human race continues to this day. It is a purpose that stretches far beyond any individual accomplishment; a purpose that reaches into the eternal future of the Kingdom. This is all we need to know about our relationship with the Father to be able to receive our inheritance and walk in our destiny.

Why then are we frustrated and restless in our walk with the Lord? Why do things not go according to plan? Many of us have a strong prophetic sense of our destiny but we often seem to fall short. Our striving is based upon a belief that we lack approval. My eyes were opened to this truth during the four years I spent in Africa. The trials and struggles that I faced during those years showed me where my heart truly was. It was only an encounter with the Father that resolved the striving of my heart. It was only when the yearning of my heart was satisfied with the love of the Father that destiny came. Today, I can honestly say that I feel more fully immersed in my prophetic destiny than ever before.

When we come into our sonship, everything else falls into place. The details of our destiny are made clear. Some may be called to serve the Body of Christ in church leadership, some in the marketplace; others are called to evangelize the lost. Whatever our calling is, we are all destined to be sons and daughters of our glorious Father. We have an inheritance that is everlasting, ruling and reigning with our brother, Jesus Christ, and bowing before the throne in worship crying, "Holy, Holy, Holy is the Lord God Almighty!" Our inheritance includes participating in the restoration of the nations and the coming of the Kingdom. Nothing can compare with that.

Once you understand your destiny as a son, receiving your inheritance follows suit. As you move from intimacy with the Father to identity as a son, then receiving your inheritance should naturally occur. However, we must not forget that this is about the heart. The Father is after our hearts, not our performances. It is so easy to fall back into trying to please the Father by doing enough to somehow prove that we are walking in our destiny. We can push ourselves to the limit in ministry only to find ourselves collapsed on the floor full of bitterness and fatigue, more confused about our destiny than ever before.

As I shared in the opening chapter, this was the very place of exasperated exhaustion that I found myself in a few years ago. I continued to lay burden upon burden upon myself by forcing things that I felt needed to happen. I sought to prove my loyalty, sacrifice, and capability in efforts to gain God's approval. I was striving so hard to reach my prophetic destiny that it nearly ruined me. In my discouragement, I questioned God, "Why can't I have my inheritance, God? I have vision and prophetic insight about where You want to take me, but I can't grasp it. I'm not in it!" I perceived my destiny, I perceived where I was called and meant to be, but it just wasn't happening.

Only after I opened up my heart to the love of the Father (Intimacy) and let Him speak over me, "My son, I love you," (Identity) could I walk in my prophetic destiny (Inheritance). Now I walk as a son, knowing that I have received the spiritual inheritance of a son. My life has never been the same since. The levels of confidence, clarity of vision, and prophetic insight are far beyond anything I experienced before. For the first time in my life I feel as though I am walking in my prophetic destiny. It is not because of how many nations I preach in, how many pastors I ordain or how many are healed when I lay my hands upon them. Rather, it is wholly rooted in the understanding within my heart that I am a son in whom Father God is well pleased.

Jesus was a Son before He became the Savior. He was destined to be the Savior but He walked as a Son in obedience to both His earthly father Joseph and His heavenly Father before He gave Himself for you and me.

His destiny was set before the beginning of time, but He had to travel the journey through intimacy and identity *before* He could complete His destiny and receive His full inheritance.

Let's pick up again with Elisha in 2 Kings 2. Elijah has been taken to heaven, and Elisha now realizes that his request for sonship, for identity, has been granted. In verses 13-14 we read:

> *"He also took up the mantle of Elijah that had fallen from him, and went back and stood by the bank of the Jordan. Then he took the mantle of Elijah that had fallen from him, and struck the water, and said, "Where is the LORD God of Elijah?" And when he also had struck the water, it was divided this way and that; and Elisha crossed over."*
>
> — 2 KINGS 2:13,14

Now that Elisha has received his identity, he is able to walk confidently and assuredly into the prophetic destiny upon his life. He was destined to carry on the prophetic calling of Elijah throughout Israel. He picks up the cloak and the spirit of Elijah comes fully upon him. These are the first steps of a man fully engaged in his prophetic purpose, exhibiting the same miraculous power as his spiritual father before him. There is clear evidence in Scripture that Elisha did twice as many miracles as Elijah before him. Elisha truly walked in his inheritance, operating in a double portion anointing as Elijah's spiritual son.

In Romans, Paul gives us another glimpse of the life of a son walking in prophetic destiny. It's a glorious place to be! Romans 8:15 reads:

> *For [the Spirit which] you have now received*
> *[is] not a spirit of slavery to put you once more*
> *in bondage to fear, but you have received*
> *the Spirit of adoption [the Spirit producing*
> *sonship] in [the bliss of] which we cry,*
> *Abba Father!*
>
> — ROMANS 8:15 (AMPLIFIED BIBLE)

You see, when we are identified as sons, there is a profound difference in the way we interact with God. All the pressure to perform is lifted off. Performance achieves nothing. We are living from a foundation of acceptance rather than trying to earn acceptance through what we do. Sons don't have to do anything to prove something to anybody, because they are *already* sons in the sight of the Father.

A son or daughter walking in his or her prophetic destiny will be found *doing* things *for* the Father. They will be riding an adventurous and expectant journey, responding to the Father's love in worshipful and surrendered service. Sons are continually listening to the Father and simply do the next thing on *His* agenda. Elisha continued the work of Elijah with countless miracles and prophetic insight, responding to the word of God as Elijah did before him. This is the inheritance established before the beginning of time; it is the ultimate freedom.

Our ability to walk in our prophetic destiny as sons holds a much weightier value than we might first imagine. The authority we carry as a result of walking in our in prophetic destiny as sons, impacts not only our personal relationship with the Father, it impacts our families and communities. Beyond that, our sonship authority holds profound implications for the earth. The earth is crying out for sons to come and bring restoration to spiritual wastelands laid barren by the fires of sin. Creation is waiting for revelation of the Kingdom. Sons and daughters must arise!

PART THREE

ANOINTED FOR
RESTORATION

CHAPTER EIGHT

WALKING IN KINGDOM AUTHORITY

≈

Authority in the Kingdom is not a consequence of position or title, but a consequence of our relationship with our Heavenly Father.

Have you ever thought about what it would have been like to live in the Garden of Eden before sin entered the world? It must have been glorious. Waters glistened in colorful spectrums of rainbows across the skies, while ferocious lions and graceful antelopes lived together in a permanent state of serenity. The clouds never grew black or poured forth rains. Tsunamis never erupted from the waters and tornadoes never spun from the sky. Drought and famine had never swept across the land. This earth was a haven for God's people to rest free from burden, a place to worship Him in unity, in spirit, and in truth.

When sin entered into the world, a cataclysmic shift occurred, not only in our ability to commune with the Father, but also in His creation. God created man with the original purpose to "rule over the fish in the sea and the birds in the sky, over the livestock and all the wild animals, and over all the creatures that move along the ground." (Genesis 1:26). Creation is meant to operate underneath the authority of man, who in turn operates underneath the authority of God. However, when man rebelled against God's authority and became dominated by the weight of sin, this curse flowed throughout creation. Creation now operates under the curse of sin and death.

This curse upon the ground is pronounced in Genesis 3:18, which reads:

> *"Cursed is the ground for your sake; In toil*
> *you shall eat of it all the days of your life. Both*
> *thorns and thistles it shall bring forth for you,*
> *and you shall eat the herb of the field."*

With the curse of sin operating among God's creation, suddenly the ground is no longer fertile. Rebellion, murder, and pride have risen up within humanity. In tandem with this, the waters are no longer pure, the seas are no longer calm, and the sky no longer silent. Just as man is now in need of salvation, so is the earth. Creation longs for reconciliation and restoration to God's original design for complete peace and unity with Him. Creation is crying out!

While the curse of sin is clearly operative among God's creation (and it continues to escalate), I do not believe that God's heart is to allow a perpetual escalation of calamitous destruction until the earth somehow implodes upon itself. I have read enough Scripture to know that God is not through with planet earth. God's heart has always been for restoration and reconciliation. This is the ministry He has given to His children (2 Corinthians 5:18).

As we have seen, the prophetic anointing, as revealed through the life of Elijah and Elisha, is always looking to restore. Jesus Christ Himself modeled this when He taught us to pray, "Your Kingdom come, Your will be done on earth as it is in heaven." (Matthew 6:10) Our ability to bring restoration to the earth and revelation of the gospel to the hearts of men can only come from the Father. Through our relationship with the Father we have the ability to know God's Kingdom purposes and live as agents and ambassadors of the Kingdom here on earth.

There is no doubt that the authority that Jesus exhibited derived from the relationship that He enjoyed with His Father. Jesus is our ultimate example of how to operate in the authority of the Father. In Mark 1:22, we see that the people "were astonished at His teaching, for He taught them as one having authority." It was the authority Jesus carried as a Son to the Father that allowed Him to speak the deeper truths of the Kingdom, to dispel demonic forces, and to calm the raging storm.

John 5:19 lays the foundation for the authority that Jesus carried:

> *"Then Jesus answered and said to them, 'Most assuredly, I say to you, the Son can do nothing of Himself, but what He sees the Father do; for whatever He does, the Son also does in like manner.'"*

The same principle is true for us. As sons of the Father, we *too* receive the ability to walk on the earth with His authority. That authority develops a prophetic desire in our hearts to reveal the Kingdom on earth as it is in heaven. Like Jesus, we pray to the Father for His will to be done, we listen to what the Father would have us do, and then do what the Father says with the confidence and authority necessary to succeed. We can do nothing of ourselves but when we see what the Father is doing, we have the ability to do it in like manner. A son's desire to see God's Kingdom manifest upon the earth provides a conduit to reveal the Father's heart.

Authority is different to power. For many years, the Church has not been short of the power needed to save the lost and heal the sick. However, I do believe that the Church has lacked in true Kingdom *authority*. What I mean by that is that we may be exerting *power*, but the power may not always be a result of hearing and seeing the Father's heart. We trail-blaze forward with our ministry agendas, only to face a lack of resources, the sapping of strength, and the demoralizing of our spirits. In the end, our ability to bring true restoration and reconciliation to the earth is limited. Kingdom *authority*, not power in numbers or resources, is what penetrates hearts with the Father's love. When you carry the authority of the Father as a son, people notice.

I heard it once said that power is the ability to act, but authority is the *right* to act. Authority is like a policeman's uniform. Once the officer clothes himself in the uniform, complete with badge and gun, he displays a whole new authority. I guarantee you that I am much more likely to stop for a man dressed in a policeman's uniform than someone wearing jeans and a T-shirt. My point here is that authority derives from our relationship with our heavenly Daddy.

For many years in Christian ministry, I struggled to see the Father supply our needs. Debt would follow us, and the perpetual state of never quite having enough placed a lot of pressure on our marriage and family. It was not as if God was unable or even reluctant to supply our needs; rather, I was an orphan believing that there was no one there to meet our needs. I would shout, speak in tongues, and quote Scripture but our breakthrough was minimal. Once the Father's presence and His love started to break into our lives, we began to see greater levels of breakthrough. The Father's love reversed my orphan thinking and, as a result, the necessity to strive became something of the past. Now, there is a new sense of authority in my prayer life. We now live debt free, both personally and in the ministry. There is no doubt that living as a son is very fruitful.

In Romans 8, we read:

> *"The Spirit Himself bears witness with our spirit that we are children of God, and if children, then heirs—heirs of God and joint heirs with Christ, if indeed we suffer with Him, that we may also be glorified together. For I consider that the sufferings of this present time are not worthy to be compared with the glory which shall be revealed in us."*
>
> — ROMANS 8:16-18

Here, in verse 18, Paul exhorts us that our present sufferings, both individually and at the level of creation, are not a permanent state of being. Rather, we see that the glory of God shall *one day* be fully revealed through us, His children, when we are clothed in righteousness and seated with His Son, Jesus, in heaven. I believe, however, that the glory will also be revealed in us *now*, on earth. Why would God only want to reveal His glory in heaven? An important part of God's design is to put His children on display to the world, as shining lights upon a hill (Matthew 5:14). This is so that all the glory of God will shine forth from us. He has called us to be His witnesses and to be lights in the world.

Ezekiel 16:1-14 portrays a prophetic picture of Jerusalem, which represents a figurative type of the Church. The final verse in the passage, verse 14, reads:

> *"Your fame went out among the nations because of your beauty, for it was perfect through My splendor which I had bestowed on you," says the Lord God."*
>
> — EZEKIEL 16:1-14

Everything within the heart of the Father longs to put us, His children, on display. We are the crown of His creation, and we are crowned in glory, not just in heaven, but also on earth. Father God desires to make His name famous among the nations, and He chooses to do it through the beauty of His relationship with His children.

Paul, in Romans, declares:

> *"For the earnest expectation of the creation eagerly waits for the revealing of the sons of God."*
>
> — ROMANS 8:19

Creation is waiting for the sons of God. Everything that God has made in His creation belongs to Him: hills, trees, mountains, valleys, seas, rivers—everything is His! But more than that, everything that God has created has a *memory*; it recognizes God. The reason it recognizes God, and has a memory of God, is because it was actually created *by* God and *for* God. Creation was created to bring God glory and pleasure. The parts of creation are made to worship God as they fulfil the purpose for which they were created. Why else would the rocks be forced to cry out if they too were not created with an innate destiny to worship the Father? (Luke 19:40)

However, now that sin has entered the world, the same disconnect that exists between us and the Father exists among creation. This is because we, as humans, carry authority over the earth. We were created to steward and cultivate the earth and its creatures in such a way as to bring glory to the Father. Now that the curse of sin operates among man, so it does in the earth.

Here is the key! Just as God is calling for reconciliation between Himself and man, so also He desires reconciliation with His entire creation. The waters, the forests, and the plains are all destined to know the Father and live in the fullness of His glory and purpose. God is calling for sons and daughters to rise up with *His* authority, His perfect and pure authority, to reveal more of God's Kingdom to this earth. When we are walking in submission to God's authority, we then hold the ability to restore the brokenness in both creation and humanity back to the Father's heart of love.

I am reluctant to enter the debate on eschatology for a variety of reasons. First and foremost, I want to keep the primary focus of my message on the salvation of Jesus Christ and the relationship we enjoy with Father God. My eschatology is based on the following certainties:

- We are part of God's end-time purpose.

- Matthew 24:14 instructs us that, "This message of the Kingdom shall be preached in all nations and then the end will come."

- There will be a pure spotless Bride at the return of Christ.

- Jesus is coming back!

The *how* of Jesus' return is up for debate. In the meantime, I would rather live as the son that I am called to be, than spend my time arguing with my brothers and sisters about how the end times will pan out.

If we take Jesus' words seriously, that the Kingdom came when He came to the earth, (Matthew 12:28, Mark 1:15, Luke 17:21), then I believe the answer is clear. The Kingdom *has come*, and it will fully come with the arrival of Jesus. In the meantime, we are to pray that the Kingdom will come on earth as it is in heaven. We are to live as children of the Kingdom, so that the world may taste how good our Father God is.

With this understanding, that the Kingdom has come and will fully come with the arrival of Jesus Christ, let us continue in Romans 8. Romans 8:19 reveals that, "...the earnest expectation of creation eagerly awaits for the revealing of the sons of God." That means that creation has to know who the sons are. Just think about it. The wind and the waves knew who Jesus was, the dead man Lazarus knew who Jesus was, and the sea that He walked on knew who Jesus was. Jesus revealed fully His authority over creation. When He was identified and released into His purpose as the Son of God, Jesus received authority over sin, sickness, disease and demons. In addition, He carried God's creative authority over nature.

When we walk as sons and daughters our authority is expanded to include the realm of nature. We should not shy away from this. Jesus Himself proclaimed that we would display even greater works than He did during His time on the earth (John 14:12). When we are walking in the authority of the Father we only do and say what the Father wants. When we are aligned with the Father, it shall be done!

If creation is going to be destroyed, as many believe, why is it looking for sons to come and bring restoration? We discover the answer in Romans 8, where Paul gives a prophetic word about the earth:

> *"For the creation was subjected to futility, not willingly, but because of Him who subjected it in hope; because the creation itself also will be delivered from the bondage of corruption into the glorious liberty of the children of God."*
>
> — ROMANS 8:20,21

Why is creation waiting for sons to come forth? Because creation knows that the only ones who have the redemptive authority to put things back into order are *sons*. God's prophetic word is that creation will be delivered from its present bondage and restored to the beauty and unified peace that existed before the fall of man. The only ones who can do that are those who walk in the full authority of the Creator. When we carry the authority of the Father, we can download the heart of the Father into the core of the earth. I think that is truly amazing!

Do you realize that our words can recreate? If Jesus could command the weather, it follows that we too, in response to the Father and through the power of the Holy Spirit, can speak to the weather. Jesus told us that we can speak to the mountains in faith and they will move (Matthew 21:21). That is why creation is looking and waiting and longing for the revealing of the sons of God. Creation responded to the authority of Christ and has a memory that will only respond to sons. Creation knows that sons can bring healing to the barren wastelands and tumultuous seas. Creation knows that sons can impart the Father's blessing of freedom from sin and death, overturning the curse by which it is currently controlled.

The earth is full of humans who have no concept of who the Father is and why He created us. They have no concept of His prophetic destiny for the earth. Orphans don't know the Father, therefore they cannot hear the Father or operate in His authority to bring restoration, reconciliation, and peace. Orphans tear apart families; they also tear apart the earth on which they dwell. Because they do not know the Father, orphans cannot pray for His kingdom to be manifested on earth.

I believe a day is coming soon when all this is going to change. As men and women, boys and girls come to a revelation of the Father's love and destiny upon their life, they will have dominion on the earth. As sons and daughters, they will come forth with an understanding of the authority they carry over the earth because of who their Daddy is and what His desire is. The Father has already declared that His purpose for the earth is to bring liberty from the bondage of sin and death. We as His sons and daughters are called to use the authority of Christ and the power of the Holy Spirit to release freedom upon the earth. This is the same freedom we have received from sin as a child of God.

Where do we see this illustrated in the life of Elijah and Elisha? After Elisha received his identity and was released into his prophetic destiny, he moved on to Jericho. But what was the first miracle released through this new life, this life as a son operating in the power and authority of his father? The first miracle Elisha did was to restore creation! In 2 Kings 2:19-22 we read:

> *"Then the men of the city (of Jericho) said to Elisha, "Please notice, the situation of this city is pleasant, as my lord sees; but the water is bad, and the ground barren."*
>
> *And he said, "Bring me a new bowl, and put salt in it." So they brought it to him. Then he went out to the source of the water, and cast in the salt there, and said, "Thus says the LORD: 'I have healed this water; from it there shall be no more death or barrenness.'" So the*

> *water remains healed to this day, according to*
> *the word of Elisha which he spoke."*

This is amazing! Elisha has just been released into full purpose and the first thing he does is take authority over the earth and bring healing to the water and the barren ground. Who knows how many lives were saved because they now had access to safe and clean water? You see, the restoration of creation ripples out and brings hope, peace, and healing to humanity as well.

The Elijah Spirit is being released upon the earth through this Agape Reformation. We are entering a magnificent season where eyes are being opened to the Father's love and more and more sons are being released. These sons will live with an understanding of the authority they carry from the Father. They will bring healing to the earth through words spoken in the power of the Holy Spirit, Hallelujah!

CHAPTER NINE

RAISING THE GENERATIONAL CEILING

≈

Our forefathers built a ceiling that has become the floor on which we live.

As we talk about walking in the kingdom authority that comes from living as a son, it is important that we understand what it means to receive a spiritual inheritance. It goes without saying that we hold no authority in ourselves. Any authority we have to manifest God's kingdom on earth can only be derived from our inheritance as sons. Just like Jesus, we receive our authority from the Father.

Spiritual inheritance also applies to other spiritual fathers in our lives. This includes our earthly, biological fathers.

I once heard Bill Johnson explain it like this. Imagine a ceiling above you. This ceiling represents the level, so to speak, that your father before you built; it speaks of the legacy that is left to you. As you step into the generational legacy of the family, you then rise to the level of that ceiling. What your father left to you becomes your starting point. In turn, you begin establishing an inheritance that will later become the floor for the generations that follow after *you*.

My point is this: *our father's ceiling becomes our floor and our starting place in life.*

God desires continuity from generation to generation. If there is a solid spiritual foundation in place, it enables us to rise higher. The spiritual blessings received are amplified from generation to generation. This is applicable to both biological *and* spiritual fathers.

This is consistently set out in Scripture. One man would build upon another man's foundations. Many men in the Old Testament were referred to using the name of their father. These men took on the identity of the father who built the floor for them.

When we consider Abraham and Isaac, we see that Isaac built upon Abraham's ceiling. In Genesis 26:18, we see that Isaac reopened the wells that Abraham had already dug. Isaac continued the work that Abraham had begun, and

God poured out His blessing. Fresh water was found, and the Lord led Isaac to Rehoboth where he declared that the Lord would give them room to flourish. Immediately after the reopening of the wells, the Lord appeared to Isaac confirming the same blessing upon his life that had been upon his father Abraham's life (Genesis 26:24). Isaac's honoring of his father's inheritance became the basis upon which God expanded *his* inheritance. Out of that, entire generations were blessed.

Jesus constantly referred back to the Father who granted Him spiritual inheritance and authority. Jesus' life and ministry was built upon that which His Father had already set in place. Jesus was *also* called the Son of David (Matthew 9:27, 15:22, 21:9). Jesus laid a ceiling through His life and ministry which then became the foundation upon which His disciples stood. When He encouraged His disciples that they would do even greater things than He did, He was, in essence, saying, "I have gone before you and laid the foundation. Now step up and continue the ministry."

Jesus' response to Simon Peter, after Peter declared Jesus as Messiah, was, "…upon this rock I will build My church." (Matthew 16:18) Simon Peter broke through the spiritual ceiling above him that had, up to that point, limited his authority and power. Jesus lifted Simon up and set him on a newly laid foundation; he was then ready to walk into a higher calling with strategic purpose and fresh authority.

In that moment Simon was given a new name, Peter, which translates to 'stone' or 'rock.' This signified his new identity and purpose. In the spiritual realm, Peter's revelation of Jesus' Messianic identity opened up his own heart and life to receiving a new identity of his own. Peter continued from that point forward with the authority needed to establish God's Church and lead God's people in the Father's Kingdom agenda.

My key point here is that Peter would have never been able to break through that ceiling unless Jesus had enabled him. Jesus was the one who established the new higher level upon which Peter desired to stand. Jesus created a ceiling so that His disciples could go further, rise higher, and stand more firmly in the immense calling upon their lives. It was Jesus' level of power and authority to which the disciples were called to rise. We see that manifest in the miracles and Kingdom impact each of them went on to make.

Jesus expressed this whole idea of a ceiling becoming a floor when He said:

> *"Most assuredly, I say to you, he who believes in Me, the works that I do he will do also; and greater works than these he will do, because I go to My Father."*
>
> — JOHN 14:12

When He spoke those words, Jesus was, in essence, saying that we will go beyond what He did and do even *greater* works. As we are obedient to walking in this spiritual inheritance, we, in turn, create ceilings that will become floors for generations following after us. As *we* accomplish the "greater works" others will fall in line with that spiritual legacy.

There are several keys to this concept of spiritual ceilings becoming floors. These are crucially important for the building process to be completed. I want to outline three specific keys.

First, *We must recognize our fathers and what they carry*.

We need spiritual eyes to see what our fathers have done and then be able to build upon that. We must be able to see who Jesus really is, just as it was pivotal for Peter to see who Jesus really was, before his (Peter's) spiritual inheritance could be fully set in place (Matthew 16:18).

1 John 1:3 tells us, "...that which we have seen and heard we declare to you, that you also may have fellowship with us; and truly our fellowship is with the Father and with His Son Jesus Christ." We cannot fully proclaim the gospel of Jesus Christ, fully embrace and walk in our spiritual inheritance as sons, unless we have first "seen and heard."

Once we recognize our fathers, whether they are biological or spiritual fathers, then we can know where to begin. Once we recognize the spiritual truth that our fathers carry, then we can pick up the mantle and walk in that same truth, blessing, and authority.

A second key concept is that: ***We must honor our fathers and be willing to lay down our lives for them.***

We must remember that our fathers have laid down their own lives for what they carry. Just as a seed planted in the ground must die before it can sprout and grow, *the spiritual seed that dies will multiply.* Jesus was commissioned to lay down His life for the Father, so that the Father's purposes could be made complete in the earth. In the same way, we are called to take up our cross (Matthew 16:34) and lay down our lives for the Father. This same principle applies within our hearts towards both our earthly and our spiritual fathers.

When I talk about laying down our life, I am referring to the call to sacrifice. Sacrificing our wants, our desires and our ideas for the sake of the spiritual inheritance that we receive and are called to release. Abraham, Isaac, David, and Jesus all sacrificed so that the generations after them could rise even higher. If a son is not willing to be like the seed that falls into the earth and dies, he curtails and hinders the inheritance that can come to him.

Look again at the transfer of identity that occurred between Elisha and Elijah in 2 Kings 2. When Elisha pleaded with Elijah to receive a double-portion of his spirit, he was essentially asking for identity and he was willing sacrifice all of himself for it. In stripping himself naked, Elisha visually enacted a powerful statement of surrender and death.

Up to that point in time, Elijah had been setting in place a foundation upon which his successor could stand and grow. This foundation consisted of complete surrender to God, hearing and doing all that God said and did. This included a level of miraculous power and prophetic anointing that was unprecedented on the earth. After receiving the double portion anointing, Elisha went on to perform twice as many miracles as Elijah. Elisha went higher and exceeded his father before him. Some have argued that this is because Elisha received twice the amount of power as Elijah. Elisha's miracles also came, however, because he was walking fully as a son, releasing more of his spiritual father's inheritance upon the earth.

The third key concept here is this: ***Carrying offense in our hearts will circumvent destiny and inheritance.***

When we are offended or hurt by a father, we are not just blocking freedom and intimacy in our relationships, we are also circumventing the inheritance which is intended to pass down the generational line. Our inheritance and destiny is hindered. Our ability to build a new floor upon our father's ceiling is vastly limited because of the offense operating within our heart.

When we are still connected to someone in unforgiveness, our heart is not free to be connected with our heavenly Father. When we rebel and cease to be our father's son or daughter, it brings a spiritual blockage to our walk with the Father. This is a sobering reality. I faced this myself a few years ago. I constantly felt rejected and disappointed from the lack of affirmation and approval from my earthly father, and consequently it hindered me in my relationship with my Father in heaven. My heart was in desperate need of healing in order for me to fully connect with Papa God and come fully into my destiny.

Father God started to show me that I was angry with my earthly father for not being affirmed in the way that I thought I should have been as a child. Throughout this season of healing I was able to give this to God, confessing my bitterness and receiving a new heart and mind. I remember the streams of His love flowing into my heart as I wept the pain away. Forgiveness is, without exception, the key to healing issues of the heart. The abiding promise from Father God was that He would now be the source of my affirmation and approval.

It was not long after this divine encounter that my parents came to visit us in California. This was a Holy Spirit set up! On the second Sunday of their visit, we all traveled to a church in Los Angeles County, where I was due to preach. On many previous occasions when I had preached with my father in attendance, I had desperately wanted his approval and affirmation. I had longed to hear him say, "I am proud of you, my son." However, those words never came and I would try to manipulate him to get him to say something good about me.

But this occasion was different. I felt free! Now Papa God was meeting the needs for love and approval in my heart. As a result, for the first time in many years, my heart felt right with my earthly father. At the end of service my father came looking for me. Standing inches away from me, he looked into my eyes and said, "I have never heard you speak like that before!" My father affirmed me like never before. It was so meaningful and touched something deep in my heart. My forgiving him had released a new grace into his heart.

The following morning, while everyone else was still asleep, my father came to me in the kitchen and asked to talk. I said, "Sure Dad, let's chat." He started by saying that God had been dealing with his heart, then he continued by asking me to forgive him for not affirming me when I was growing up. I was blown away! I looked into his eyes and said, "Dad, you are forgiven." It was an amazing and deeply poignant moment between us. Something incredibly deep happened in both our hearts.

Today, I have a great relationship with my father. I love him and my mother so much; they have been an amazing blessing in my life. My father and I can talk like we are the best of friends. We are open and vulnerable with each other and always have loads of fun together. You see, my father built a ceiling for me. He has been in ministry since his early twenties and now, in his eighties, he is still preaching and ministering the gospel. I repeat what I said earlier. We have two fathers, a Father who is perfect, and a father who is imperfect, but *still a father. How we honor the imperfect father will determine our relationship with the perfect Father.*

Our ministry today builds upon the ceiling that my father established. I am his seed. Unlike me, you may not have had any Christian influence or heritage in your life. That does not mean you cannot honor and build up what your parents have given to you. My wife's family has no recent identifiable Christian heritage, however, Gunilla has a very strong value of honesty, respect for life and integrity that is obviously an inherited characteristic. Now, with God's help, she is building on the ceiling that was given to her. She is also partnering with me in raising the floor for our own children.

It is our connection with both our earthly and heavenly

fathers that determines our destiny. Without a healthy and whole relationship with our earthly fathers, *as far as it depends on us*, we will never be able to move beyond the affirmation and identity that we crave in the human sense in order to receive the deeper affirmation and identity that comes as a spiritual son or daughter. As we have said earlier, it is intimacy that leads to identity and moves on to destiny. Lack of intimacy with our Father means no identity as a son. No identity, then no destiny!

Elijah set a ceiling of greater intimacy with the Father. That ceiling of prophetic destiny would establish a foundation for whoever followed in his generational legacy. Elijah's ministry created a generational ceiling allowing Elisha to go even further in the prophetic destiny and anointing upon *his* life. This ceiling created a new and higher foundation upon which Elisha could stand, one that reached closer to the Father's heart. A generational torch had been passed on. The passion and power that initially flamed within Elijah's heart was now set ablaze within his son, Elisha.

What does this mean for each of us? What is the generational ceiling above your life? What foundation has your own earthly father set? Is your father in a passionate pursuit of love and surrender to our Father God? Perhaps your father is weighed down and restricted by burdens of shame, fear or recurring sin. There could be father-wounds operating that reach back through generations, which are now subverting your own ability to enjoy intimacy with the Father.

No human is able to lay a perfect platform upon which the generations following can stand. Our foundations are cracked and vulnerable to the shame and sin that permeate our hearts. However, as we come to a more full revelation of the Father, we open up the way for a new foundation to be laid. As we allow the Father to embrace our hearts, He mends the wounds that have kept us bound to the lower levels beneath. The Father reaches out His arms of love and lifts us up to a higher destiny, a richer heritage, and levels of blessing and anointing we are yet to discover.

CHAPTER TEN

THE FINAL
FRONTIER

~

"Ask of me and I will give the nations as your inheritance, the ends of the earth for your possession."

— PSALM 2:8

It is my conviction that one of the final frontiers, if not *the* final frontier, is the gospel penetrating the Muslim world. We are currently seeing Muslim people in nations such as Iran and Pakistan experiencing revival in record proportions. Hundreds are being baptized monthly, vibrant churches are being raised up, and countless Muslims are having dreams and visitations from Jesus. Some have even testified to a physical encounter with Jesus that resulted in conversion. There is no doubt that the Father is pursuing the

Muslim people and working in an amazing way throughout the Middle-Eastern nations.

However, in contrast with this, Muslim nations have sought to strongly resist the Gospel extending throughout the earth. This resistance is not solely a result of the radical militancy that we see on the news. These outbursts of extremism reveal a deeper spiritual dynamic operating within Islam itself. The rage, radicalism, and subsequent persecution of Christians by Muslims is rooted in the book of Genesis.

Do you realize that Abraham, the father of many nations (Genesis 17:5), is also the father of the Muslim peoples? Ishmael, who was born of the maidservant, Hagar (as a consequence of Abraham's distrust of God) subsequently became the father of the Muslim people. Muslims and Jews, as well as Christians, are brothers and sisters torn apart by the detrimental consequences of Abraham and Sarah's sin. It is heartbreaking to grasp how all the war, suffering and persecution ultimately boils down to the broken relationship between parents and children. Abraham truly became the father of many nations, and these nations were meant to be united as one people, not to live as fierce enemies.

In Genesis 21, we read of Hagar and her son Ishmael being cast out of Abraham's household and banished to the wilderness:

> *"So Abraham rose early in the morning, and
> took bread and a skin of water; and putting
> it on her shoulder, he gave it and the boy to
> Hagar, and sent her away. Then she departed
> and wandered in the Wilderness of Beersheba.
> And the water in the skin was used up, and
> she placed the boy under one of the shrubs.
> Then she went and sat down across from him
> at a distance of about a bowshot; for she said
> to herself, "Let me not see the death of the
> boy." So she sat opposite him, and lifted her
> voice and wept."*
>
> — GENESIS 21:14-16

Here is a mother left void of all hope of survival for
herself or her son. Rather than watch her son die from
dehydration, she places him beneath a bush to die. Can
you imagine how Ishmael must have felt throughout these
tragic and seemingly fatal last moments? Ishmael was most
likely a teenager, perhaps 16 or 17 years old, and had lived
and served among his father's household for his entire life.
He was rejected, cut off from the family and stripped of the
inheritance reserved for the firstborn son. Ishmael was no
longer a son, but was now, to all intents and purposes, an
orphan. All that lay before him was a slow and agonizing
death and it came at the word of his father. No words can
fully describe the pain that must have been welling up
within Ishmael's heart and soul.

There is no doubt that when Ishmael was cast out of his father's house there were spirits of rejection and unworthiness that took root in his heart. Within Ishmael, a father-wound of magnificent proportions grew, a wound that he would naturally carry as a result of the rejection experienced at the hands of his father, Abraham. This sense of rejection grew to bitter jealousy and, ultimately, to an insatiable desire for retaliation against his younger brother. While these spirits were not fully manifested in Isaac and Ishmael's day, today we are witnessing the full effects as Islam and Judaism exist beneath a cloud of dangerous hostility against one another.

The rejection that Abraham extended Ishmael and, by extension, to the Muslim people, has created a culture controlled and dominated by an orphan spirit. It is crucial that we, as Christians, have a clear understanding that the Father's love has the ability to heal father-wounds. When we walk as sons and daughters in the full revelation of the Father's love, we are given an authority and a special measure of grace to reach out to Muslims with a love that they have never experienced. We can restore and reconcile the brokenness that has plagued them from the time of Abraham to this very day. This is the power of the gospel, the power of the Father's love, that we carry as His children.

This, in essence, is the message I desire to communicate to you. When you look at the aggression that is coming from the Muslim world, it is significantly correlated to injustice.

Anyone that carries the sort of father-wound found within the history of the Muslim people is carrying a grievance in their heart. You see this clearly in the Muslim view of God. Allah (Arabic for 'God') is portrayed as harsh, temperamental, and impersonal. This stands in stark contrast to the loving, heavenly Daddy that we know. Our God is a loving, gracious Father who longs for relationship. That is why He created us and He pursues us with His love.

Let me draw this all together in the context of the Elijah Spirit. Remember that the Elijah Spirit is a fathering spirit that releases the spirit of sonship into our hearts. This spirit of sonship gives us prophetic destiny and eternal inheritance. I shared earlier that I believe the reference to the Elijah Spirit coming in Malachi 4:5-6 was not only a prophetic word fulfilled through John the Baptist. It is also a prophetic word applicable to the second coming of Christ. I truly believe that the Elijah (fathering) Spirit will be released upon the earth before the return of Jesus, and it will be the key to unlock the seemingly impenetrable hearts of many Muslims.

Isn't it remarkable that the Muslim nations really are the last frontier? The tumultuous events occurring throughout the Middle East are no coincidence. The 'Arab Spring' was no coincidence! God is shaking many nations across the Middle East, preparing the hearts of Muslims across the world to receive a revelation of His love. The Holy Spirit of Sonship has to be released into their hearts so that the generational wounds that have plagued Ishmael's lineage throughout history may be healed.

Finally, let me share one other exhilarating component of this release of the Father's love. I also believe that numerous Jews are going to come to faith in Christ Jesus, and are already coming to faith, as the Muslim world embraces the Gospel. As their generational brothers see the Father, they too will see God the Father. God's family will be complete and we will truly see the fullness of the Kingdom on earth as in heaven. Hallelujah!

> *Father, I thank You today for Your amazing love that baptizes my heart. You have always pursued me and continually loved me. Thank You that it is Your love that changes me and restores my heart, allowing Your resemblance to manifest itself through my life. Thank You, Father, that You call me Your son/Your daughter and that I get to walk with You as Jesus walked with You. Father, I continually give You permission to be my Father and father my heart in Your love and presence.*

STAY IN TOUCH...

For more details about the ministry and
upcoming events, please visit the website at
www.revivaltothenations.org

PO Box 13058,
San Bernardino,
CA 92423, USA

Made in the USA
Columbia, SC
09 July 2018